Practicing Organization Development

**The Change Agent Series
for Groups and Organizations**

MISSION STATEMENT

The books in this series are intended to be cutting-edge, state-of-the-art, and innovative approaches to participative change in organizational settings. They are written for, and written by, organization development (OD) practitioners interested in new approaches to facilitating participative change. They are geared to providing both theory and advice on practical application.

SERIES EDITORS

**William J. Rothwell
Roland Sullivan
Kristine Quade**

EDITORIAL BOARD

**David Bradford
W. Warner Burke
Edie Seashore
Robert Tannenbaum
Christopher Worley
Shaolin Zhang**

Beyond
Change
Management

Beyond Change Management

Advanced Strategies for Today's Transformational Leaders

Dean Anderson
Linda S. Ackerman Anderson

Pfeiffer
A Wiley Imprint
www.pfeiffer.com

Practicing
Organization
Development

Published by

JOSSEY-BASS/PFEIFFER

A Wiley Company
989 Market Street
San Francisco, CA 94103-1741
415.433.1740; Fax 415.433.0499
800.274.4434; Fax 800.569.0443

www.pfeiffer.com

Jossey-Bass/Pfeiffer is a registered trademark of John Wiley & Sons, Inc.

ISBN: 0-7879-5645-7
Library of Congress Catalog Card Number 00-011970

Library of Congress Cataloging-in-Publication Data

Anderson, Dean, 1953-
  Beyond change management : advanced strategies for today's
transformational leaders / Dean Anderson, Linda S. Ackerman
Anderson.
    p. cm.—(The Practicing organization development
series)
  ISBN 0-7879-5645-7
  1. Leadership. 2. Organizational change. I.
Ackerman Anderson, Linda S., 1950- II. Title. III. Series.
  HD57.7 .D522 2001
  658.4'063—dc21

                                         00-011970

Acquiring Editor: Matthew Holt
Director of Development: Kathleen Dolan Davies
Developmental Editor: Susan Rachmeler
Editor: Rebecca Taff

Senior Production Editor: Dawn Kilgore
Manufacturing Manager: Becky Carreño
Interior and Cover Design: Bruce Lundquist
Illustrations: Richard Sheppard

Printed in the United States of America

Printing 10 9 8 7 6 5 4 3

We at Jossey-Bass strive to use the most environmentally sensitive paper stocks available to us. Our publications are printed on acid-free recycled stock whenever possible, and our paper always meets or exceeds minimum GPO and EPA requirements.

Contents

Section One
A Call for Conscious Transformation

Section Two
Mindset: The Leverage Point for Transformation

Section Three
A Process Orientation for Leading Transformation

Section Four
Conscious Transformational Leadership

List of Tables,
Figures,
and Exhibits

Foreword
to the Series

ON **1967,** Warren Bennis, Ed Schein, and I were faculty members of the Sloan School of Management at MIT. We decided to produce a series of paperback books that collectively would describe the state of the field of organization development (OD). Organization development as a field had been named by myself and several others from our pioneer change effort at General Mills in Minneapolis, Minnesota, some ten years earlier.

Today I define OD as "a systemic and systematic change effort, using behavioral science knowledge and skill, to transform the organization to a new state."

In any case, several books and many articles had been written, but there was no consensus on whether OD was a field of practice, an area of study, or a profession. We had not even established OD as a theory or even as a practice.

We decided that there was a need for something that would describe the state of OD. Our intention was to each write a book and also to recruit three other authors. After some searching, we found a young editor who had just joined the small publishing house of Addison-Wesley. We made contact, and the series was born. Our audience was to be human resource professionals who spent their time consulting with managers in their development through various small-group activities, such as team building. More than thirty books have been published in that series, and the series has had a life of its own. We just celebrated its thirtieth anniversary.

At last year's National OD Network Conference, I said that it was time for the OD profession to change and transform itself. Is that not what we change agents tell our clients to do? This new Jossey-Bass/Pfeiffer series will do just that. It can be seen as:

- A documentation of the re-invention of OD;

- An effort that will take us to the next level; and

- A practical effort to transfer to the world the theory and practice of leading-edge practitioners and theorists.

The books in this new series will thus prove to be valuable resources for change agents to keep current with the new and leading-edge ideas and practices.

May this very exciting change agent series be most creative and innovative. May it give our field a renewed burst of energy and awareness.

Richard Beckhard
Written on Labor Day weekend 1999 from my summer cabin near Bethel, Maine

Introduction
to the Series

"We must become the change we want to see."

—Mahatma Gandhi

"We live in a moment of history where change is so speeded up that we begin to see the present only when it is already disappearing."

—R. D. Laing

WE CAN EXPECT MORE CHANGE to occur in our lifetimes than has occurred since the beginning of civilization over ten thousand years ago. *Practicing Organization Development: The Change Agent Series for Groups and Organizations* is a new series of books being launched to help those who must cope with or create change in organizational settings. That includes almost everyone.

The Current State of Organization Development

Our view of OD in this series is an optimistic one. We believe that OD is gaining favor as decision makers realize that a balance *must* be struck between the drivers of change and the people involved in it and affected by it. Although OD does have

its disadvantages at a time characterized by quantum leap change, it remains prefer-
able to such alternative approaches to change as coercion, persuasion, leadership
change, and debate.[1] Organization development practitioners are reinventing their
approaches, based on certain foundational roots of the field, in combination with
emerging principles to ensure that OD will increasingly be recognized as a viable,
important, and inherently participative approach to help people in organizations
facilitate, anticipate, and manage change.

A Brief History of the Genesis of the OD Series

A few years ago, and as a direct result of the success of *Practicing Organization Development: A Guide for Practitioners* by Rothwell, Sullivan, and McLean, the publisher—
feeling that OD was experiencing a rebirth of interest in the United States and in
other nations—wanted to launch a new OD series. The goal of this new series was
not to replace, or even compete directly with, the well-established Addison-Wesley
OD Series (edited by Edgar Schein). Instead, as the editors saw it, this series would
provide a means by which the most promising authors in OD whose voices had not
previously been heard could share their ideas. The publisher enlisted the support
of Bill Rothwell, Roland Sullivan, and Kristine Quade to turn the dream of a series
into a reality.

This series was long in the making. After sharing many discussions with the
publisher and circulating among themselves several draft descriptions of the series
editorial guidelines, the editors were guests of Bob Tannenbaum, one of the field's
founders, in Carmel, California, in February 1999 to discuss the series with a group
of well-known OD practitioners interested in authoring books. Several especially
supportive publisher representatives, including Matt Holt and Josh Blatter, were
also present at that weekend-long meeting. It was an opportunity for diverse OD
practitioners, representing many philosophical viewpoints, to come together to
share their vision for a new book series. In a sense, this series represents an OD intervention in the OD field in that it is geared to bringing change to the field most closely
associated with change management and facilitation.

---

[1]W. Rothwell, R. Sullivan, & G. McLean. (1995). Introduction (pp. 3–46). In W. Rothwell, R. Sullivan, &
G. McLean, *Practicing Organization Development: A Guide for Consultants*. San Francisco, CA: Jossey-Bass/
Pfeiffer.

What Distinguishes the Books in this Series

The books in this series are meant to be cutting-edge and state-of-the-art in their approach to OD. The goal of the series is to provide an outlet for proven authorities in OD who have not put their ideas into print or for up-and-coming writers in OD who have new, sometimes unorthodox, approaches that are stimulating and exciting. Some of the books in this series describe inspirational concepts that can lead to actionable change and purvey ideas so new that they are not fully developed.

Unique to this series is the cutting-edge emphasis, the immediate applicability, and the ease of transferability of the concepts. The aim of this series is nothing less than to reinvent, re-energize, and reinvigorate OD. In each book, we have also recommended that the author(s) provide:

- A research base of some kind, meaning new information derived from practice and/or systematic investigation and

- Practical tools, worksheets, case studies and other ready-to-go approaches that help the authors drag "theory" to "practice" to make these new, cutting-edge approaches more concrete.

Subject Matter That Will (and Will Not) Be Covered

The books in this series are varied in their approach, but they are united by their focus. All share an emphasis on organization development (OD). Hence, books in this series are about participative change efforts. They are not about such other popular topics as leadership, management development, consulting, group dynamics—unless those topics are treated in new, cutting-edge ways and are geared to OD practitioners.

This Book

Beyond Change Management wakes leaders and consultants up to what it actually takes to lead and consult to transformational change successfully.

This book highlights the missing ingredients in current change management practices and reveals the neglected people and process dynamics that so often cause failure in change. In compelling fashion, the book demonstrates the requirement that leaders become much more conscious of these unseen dynamics, which enables them to create an integrated, process-oriented, change strategy. The book introduces the new change leadership competency of process thinking and spotlights leader and employee mindset change as a key driver of successful transformation. *Beyond Change Management* sets the conceptual stage for the pragmatic guidance offered in the authors' companion book in this series, *The Change Leader's Roadmap*.

Series Website

For further information and resources about the books in this series and about the current and future practice of organization development, we encourage readers to visit the series website at *www.PracticingOD.Pfeiffer.com*.

William J. Rothwell
University Park, PA

Roland Sullivan
Deephaven, MN

Kristine Quade
Minnetonka, MN

Statement
of the Board

OT IS OUR PLEASURE TO PARTICIPATE in and influence the start up of *Practicing Organization Development: The Change Agent Series for Groups and Organizations.* The purpose of the series is to stimulate the profession and influence how OD is defined and practiced. This statement is intended to set the context for the series by addressing three important questions: (1) What is OD? (2) Is the OD profession at a crossroads? and (3) What is the purpose of this series?

What Is Organization Development?

We offer the following definition of OD to stimulate debate:

> Organization development is a system-wide and values-based collaborative process of applying behavioral science knowledge to the adaptive development, improvement, and reinforcement of such organizational features as the strategies, structures, processes, people, and cultures that lead to organization effectiveness.

The definition suggests that OD can be understood in terms of its several foci:

First, *OD is a system-wide process.* It works with whole systems. In the past, the bias has been toward working at the individual and group levels. More recently, the focus has shifted to organizations and multi-organization systems. We support that trend in general but honor and acknowledge the fact that the traditional focus on smaller systems is both legitimate and necessary.

Second, *OD is values-based.* Traditionally, OD has attempted to distinguish itself from other forms of planned change and applied behavioral science by promoting a set of humanistic values and by emphasizing the importance of personal growth as a key to its practice. Today, that focus is blurred and there is much debate about the value base underlying the practice of OD. We support a more formal and direct conversation about what these values are and how the field is related to them.

Third, *OD is collaborative.* Our first value commitment as OD practitioners is to bring about an inclusive, diverse workforce with a focus of integrating differences into a world-wide culture mentality.

Fourth, *OD is based on behavioral science knowledge.* Organization development should incorporate and apply knowledge from sociology, psychology, anthropology, technology, and economics toward the end of making systems more effective. We support the continued emphasis in OD on behavioral science knowledge and believe that OD practitioners should be widely read and comfortable with several of the disciplines.

Fifth, *OD is concerned with the adaptive development, improvement, and reinforcement of strategies, structures, processes, people, culture, and other features of organizational life.* This statement not only describes the organizational elements that are the target of change, but also describes the process by which effectiveness is increased. That is, OD works in a variety of areas, and it is focused on improving these areas. We believe that such a statement of process and content strongly implies that a key feature of OD is the transference of knowledge and skill to the system so that it is more able to handle and manage change in the future.

Sixth and finally, *OD is about improving organization effectiveness.* It is not just about making people happy; it is also concerned with meeting financial goals, improving productivity, and addressing stakeholder satisfaction. We believe that OD's future is closely tied to the incorporation of this value in its purpose and the demonstration of this objective in its practice.

Is the OD Profession at a Crossroads?

For years, OD professionals have said that OD is at a crossroads. From our perspective at the beginning of the new millennium, the field of organization development can be characterized by the following statements:

1. Practitioners today are torn. The professional organizations representing OD practitioners, including the OD Network, the OD Institute, the International OD Association, and the Academy of Management's OD and Change Division, are experiencing tremendous uncertainties in their purposes, practices, and relationships.

2. There are increasing calls for regulation/certification.

3. Many respected practitioners have suggested that people who profess to manage change are behind those who are creating it. Organization development practitioners should lead through influence rather than follow the lead of those who are sometimes coercive in their approach to change.

4. The field is defined by techniques.

5. The values that guide the field are unclear and ill-defined.

6. Too many people are practicing OD without any training in the field.

7. Practitioners are having difficulty figuring out how to market their services.

The situation suggests the following provocative questions:

- How can OD practitioners help formulate strategy, shape the strategy development process, contribute to the content of strategy, and drive how strategy will be implemented?

- How can OD practitioners encourage an open examination of the ways organizations are conceived and managed?

- How can OD focus on the drivers of change external to individuals, such as the external environment, business strategy, organization change, and culture change, as well as on the drivers of change internal to individuals, such as individual interpretations of culture, behavior, style, and mindset?

- How much should OD be part of the competencies of all leaders and how much should it be the sole domain of professionally trained, career-oriented OD practitioners?

What Is the Purpose of This Series?

This series is intended to provide current thinking about OD as a field and to provide practical approaches based on sound theory and research. It is targeted for full-time external or internal OD practitioners; top executives in charge of enterprise-wide change; and managers, HR practitioners, training and development professionals, and others who have responsibility for change in organizational and trans-organizational settings. At the same time, these books will be directed toward cutting-edge thinking and state-of-the-art approaches. In some cases, the ideas, approaches, or techniques described are still evolving, so the books are intended to open up dialogue.

We know that the books in this series will provide a leading forum for thought-provoking dialogue within the OD field.

About the Board Members

David Bradford is senior lecturer in organizational behavior at the Graduate School of Business, Stanford University, Palo Alto, California. He is co-author (with Allan R. Cohen) of *Managing for Excellence, Influence Without Authority*, and *POWER UP: Transforming Organizations Through Shared Leadership*.

W. Warner Burke is professor of psychology and education and chair of the Department of Organization and Leadership at Teachers College, Columbia University, New York, New York. His most recent publication is *Business Profiles of Climate Shifts: Profiles of Change Makers*, (with William Trahant and Richard Koonce).

Edith Whitfield Seashore is organization consultant and co-founder (with Morley Segal) of AUNTL Masters Program in Organization Development. She is co-author of *What Did You Say?* and *The Art of Giving and Receiving Feedback* and co-editor of *The Promise of Diversity*.

Robert Tannenbaum is emeritus professor of development of human systems, Graduate School of Management, University of California, Los Angeles; recipient of Lifetime Achievement Award by the National OD Network. He has published numerous books, including *Human Systems Development* with Newton Margulies and Fred Massarik.

Christopher G. Worley is director, MSOD Program, Pepperdine University, Malibu, California. He is co-author of *Organization Development and Change* (7th ed.), with Tom Cummings, and of *Integrated Strategic Change*, with David Hitchin and Walter Ross.

Shaolin Zhang is senior manager of organization development for Motorola (China) Electronics Ltd. He received his master's degree in American Studies from Beijing Foreign Studies University, Beijing, China, and holds a Ph.D. in sociology from York University, Toronto, Canada.

To Terra—for being the loving inspiration in both of our lives

Preface

OUR LIFE'S WORK HAS ALWAYS BEEN ABOUT CHANGE, Dean's about personal change and Linda's about organization change. In 1986, when we met, it became clear that our two professional specialties were meant to be merged into one unified approach to transforming organizations.

Dean was one of the first people doing personal mastery work in organizations, having created the Optimal Performance Institute to offer his approach to breakthrough performance (originally developed for world-class athletes) to people in business. Linda was one of the founding leaders of the Organization Transformation movement, focusing on teaching the process of organization change and transformational leadership to executives and consultants worldwide. At the time of our meeting, Dean had realized that his personal and team performance models had to align with the complexities of larger organizational systems, while Linda had recognized that her work required more overt emphasis on personal and cultural change to fortify her large systems work.

In 1988, we brought our specialties, insights, and theories together to create our approach to leading conscious transformation and to form Being First, Inc.

For fourteen years, we have mentored and coached one another in our individual specialties, and we now stand as peers in both arenas—personal and organizational change.

Individually, and then collectively at Being First, we have always considered ourselves thought leaders in the field of organization change. We have helped define the field of Organization Transformation and are committed to pushing the envelope of thinking and practice for accomplishing tangible, transformational results. We created Being First—appropriately named for our bias toward the personal work required to transform individuals and organizations—to offer our thinking and advice to people and large systems around the world.

Today, Being First, Inc., is a full-service change education, consulting, and change leadership development firm assisting organizations to design and accomplish their transformations while building their internal capacity for continuous change. We provide enterprise-wide breakthrough training for culture and mindset change, personal transformation training, change strategy consulting, change leadership skill development for leaders and consultants, licensing of our Change Process Methodology, coaching, and transformational team development. We offer consulting guidance, consultant support, and application tools to design and implement transformational change consciously. We are also developing a curriculum for women executives called "Women As Leaders of Change."

Our style, based on our commitment to walk our own talk, is to co-create a personalized strategy for each client with the appropriate balance of consulting and training, combining both change for the individual employee and change for the system as a whole. We are devoted to our own continuous learning through true partnership with our clients. We hope this way of working is evident in what we offer in this book.

Our work in organizations continues to provide us the opportunity to develop, field test, and write about what we believe is required to transform human systems successfully and consciously. Through our practice, as well as in the current management literature, it has become clear that several essential messages and competencies are missing from the field. These need to be given voice. Some are about how leaders lead profound change in their organizations. Some concern consultants and their approaches or ability to influence their clients as change leaders. We deeply believe that leaders and consultants need to hear these messages and develop these competencies in order to transform their organizations to stay in sync with their rapidly changing environments. We have attempted to articulate clearly both the messages and the competencies in this book and its companion, *The Change Leader's Roadmap.*

Through writing these books, we have attempted to capture what is true for us in this moment in time in the evolution of change and leadership. This has been a challenging effort—a bit like trying to capture a river that keeps on flowing. The insights we explore here will continue to evolve—and have done so even as we have written them. We explore ideas and theory at the conceptual level, offer strategies, actions, and tools at the pragmatic level, and attempt to bridge the two in the clearest and most useful way possible for you, our reader.

For two decades, we have thoroughly danced the debate of personal change versus organization change, change the people or change the structures, plan versus unfold, process versus outcome. The dances continue, and we offer you where we currently stand. In our writing, we have attempted to be forthright about what we see as true about how the nature of change and leadership are evolving. We have also attempted to denote what we think is factual, what we believe due to our own experiences, and what we are still learning or questioning.

We are very much on the continuing journey of inquiry, discovery, and adaptation of what we think and feel about what we have written here. We invite you, our reader, into this exploration with us—into the inquiry—into our attempt to give language, guidance, and incentive to growing the field of transformational change leadership. We hope you will participate in the conversation about the issues and propositions in these books, if not put them into practice to reap their value.

Please read on with the spirit of inquiry. Read with your concern for the state of today's organizations. Read to contribute to our collective ability to transform organizations into places in which people love to work and feel regenerated, as well as adding value to their customers or constituents. Read on while honoring how far the field of organization development has come from its first attempts to infuse the notions and values of planned change and human development into organizations. And please read with yourself in mind as a leader or consultant of change. Our message is written for you, and we hope it benefits you personally and professionally.

Dean Anderson
Linda S. Ackerman Anderson
Durango, Colorado
Summer 2000

Acknowledgments

WE EXPRESS OUR DEEP APPRECIATION for all of the people who helped us write and produce both *Beyond Change Management* and *The Change Leader's Roadmap*. Completing these books was very much a group effort. We received tremendous support from our families and friends, while we took on the challenge of writing two books simultaneously—and completing them.

Above all, we appreciate our young daughter, Terra, whose heartfelt understanding and patience for the time and focus these books required of us was essential to our process. Her smiles and gentle offerings of help and support provided food for our souls, and her reminders that there was more to life than writing created humbling perspective for our prolonged effort. And we appreciate one another for being such a full partner in co-creating our relationship, lives and work. We are in awe of the process we are living—consciously listening to Spirit, accepting our humanness, and surrendering ourselves and our relationship to the fire of transformation.

We received direct help from our trusty readers, friends and colleagues all, including insightful input from John Adams, Carol Tisson, Jean Redfield, and, of course, our series editors, Kristine Quade, Roland Sullivan, and William Rothwell. Their feedback and encouragement was invaluable to us, as was that of our Pfeiffer editors.

Our staff was untiring in their assistance with editing and production. We sincerely appreciate Cindy Lancaster, Orion Lukasik, Marilyn Leftwich, Steve Elfrink, Lisa Liljedahl, Kevin Smith, and Cindy Marquardt for their dedication and patience.

In addition, we appreciate all of our Being First, Inc., consulting and training associates for being the road warriors who kept our clients happy while we wrote for so many months. For this, we are deeply grateful.

And finally, we appreciate Martin Marquardt for his partnership, friendship, and positive influence on our thinking over the years.

Beyond
Change
Management

Introduction

WE CAN REMEMBER WHEN CHANGE CONSULTANTS were few and far between. About the only people thinking about and promoting planned change back then were a handful of organization development practitioners, and they seldom captured the attention of senior leaders.

As we enter the 21st Century, change and how to lead it successfully has become the foremost topic on the minds of organizational leaders. And for good reasons: Change is happening everywhere; its speed and complexity are increasing; and the future success of our organizations depends on how successful leaders are at leading that change. In today's marketplace, change is a *requirement* for continued success, and competent change leadership is a most coveted executive skill.

Organizations' track records at change are not very good. The vast majority of today's change efforts are failing to produce their intended business results. These struggling efforts are producing huge cost to budgets, time, people, customers, and faith in leadership. Organizations are spending tens of millions of dollars on change efforts such as reengineering and information technology

1

installations, yet not obtaining their intended return on investment. Furthermore, the very methods used in these failed efforts are causing tremendous resistance and burnout in people, loss of employee morale, and turmoil in the cultures of organizations. Put simply, organizational leaders are falling short in their efforts to lead change successfully.

Over the past fifteen years, technology and other marketplace drivers have radically altered the very nature of change itself. Whereas change was once a contained transactional event (and easier to manage), it is now more open-ended, radical, complex, personal, and continuous. "Transformation" is the new type of change that has emerged, and it is by far the most prevalent and complex type occurring in organizations today. In general, leaders do not understand transformational change or how to lead it, which is causing virtually all of the change-related problems they are now facing.

Over the past decade or so, these struggles have given rise to the field of change management. For the most part, change management practitioners have attempted to provide solutions to two major problems—how to plan better for implementation and how to overcome employee resistance. However, these two necessary components of change have not produced adequate positive results, especially for transformational change. Why? Because attention to implementation and resistance is only the tip of the iceberg of what is required in transformation. It is now time to move beyond change management into change leadership, now time to develop the advanced change strategies that support this new type of change.

Leaders in need of change assistance have always been a window of professional opportunity for organization development (OD) and change management consultants. However, for the most part, these practitioners have not been as effective at providing the necessary support and guidance to organizational leaders as is necessary for transformational change. Put bluntly, most change consultants need to expand their awareness, skills, and approaches to leading transformational change as well.

What is the source of the problem? Is the issue about the changing nature of change? Is it about leadership? Or is it about organization development and change management consulting practices? *Our premise is that it is about all three: change, leadership, and today's consulting approaches.*

Transformational change involves a number of very critical and unique dynamics that demand a new leadership perspective, skill, and style. Most leaders, however, are viewing transformation through their old perspectives and are applying traditional management approaches that just don't work. Because leading transformational change is so radically different from managing or leading a stable organization, leaders cannot simply lay their old way of thinking, behaving, and operating on this new world and expect success.

Leading transformation calls for a deeper understanding of change and a new set of leadership skills and strategies. Leaders must broaden their understanding and insight about what transformational change requires, let go of or build off of their old approaches, and guide the process of transformation differently. In particular, they must transform their beliefs about people, organizations, and change itself; they must view transformation through a new set of mental lenses in order to see the actual dynamics of transformation; and they must alter their leadership style and behavior to accommodate the unique requirements of transformation.

This means that leaders themselves must transform in order to lead transformation successfully in their organizations. Only then will the new skills of transformational change leadership become available to them. Only then will they be able to see, understand, and apply the strategies and approaches that make transformation work. And only then will they want to.

This is not to say that leaders are bad, wrong, unskilled, or somehow flawed. In fact, quite the contrary. Over the past two decades, leaders have done a phenomenal job of increasing the productivity of their organizations. However, because today's change is so often transformational (making it much more complex), the requirements for today's leaders, out of necessity, are expanding. The challenge is that today's marketplace is not asking for just leadership. It is demanding *change leadership*—even more, *transformational change leadership*—a new breed of leader for a new breed of change.

Leaders are doing their best at leading change, given the training and experience they have had. Over the past few decades, organizations have put tremendous resources into turning their managers into leaders. Now, they must dedicate even more resources to turning those leaders into change leaders who can successfully lead the transformation of their organizations.

Organization development consultants must be there to assist. However, to play this critical coaching role, OD consultants must also deepen their own understanding of transformation, both personal and organizational, to become true experts in the field of transformation.

Over the years, OD has had tremendous impact on organizational performance with traditional approaches such as team building, survey feedback, work redesign, cultural audits, and vision and values clarification. But this work over the years has been mostly piecemeal and has seldom been applied system-wide as a part of a consciously designed, long-term process of change.

Transformation requires OD consultants to broaden, deepen, and integrate their approaches to change. In short, OD consultants must evolve the process skills of their profession to better serve the needs of 21st Century change transformation. They must take a larger view of what is needed in the organization—a whole-systems, long-term, process perspective. Furthermore, OD consultants must become better skilled at the intra-psychic and interpersonal dynamics of human transformation and learn to integrate these "people processes" with the systems dynamics of large scale organization transformation.

In the past, OD consultants have been content to provide service when their clients have allowed them; now, they must find ways to alter how they are viewed by their clients so they can have greater influence on larger, whole system change efforts. Where they have been reactive, OD consultants must now be proactive and deliver new strategies and tools that meet the unique needs of transformation.

We believe that both leaders and consultants need a breakthrough to what we call "conscious transformation." The term "conscious" signifies a required shift in both leaders' and consultants' "consciousness" regarding how they view change, themselves, and their roles as change leaders. Let's explore the terms.

Webster's dictionary defines *"conscious"* as "to know, awareness of an inward state or outward fact; perceiving, noticing with a degree of controlled thought or observation; capable of thought, will, design and perception; acting with critical awareness."

Webster defines *"consciousness"* as "awareness, especially of something within oneself, and also the state of being conscious of an external object, state, or fact; the state of being characterized by sensation, emotion, volition, and thought; the upper level of mental life as contrasted with unconscious processes; mindfulness."

"Transformation" implies a quantum change in form, nature, or function. *Conscious transformation,* then, infers that leaders and consultants alike must become more "conscious" and aware of the deeper and more subtle dynamics of transformation, both personal (including their own) and organizational (including the organization's strategy and systems dynamics unique to transformation). This increased awareness is the starting point for leaders and consultants to increase their change leadership skills.

A Multi-Dimensional Approach to Mastering Change Leadership

Mastery of any skill requires that you develop all aspects of the task. You cannot specialize in one area and neglect the others. For example, to be a masterful communicator, you must develop both speaking and listening skills. Masterful golfers must be able to hit both the long ball and the short ball well. Masterful parents must know how to discipline as well as how to nurture their children. Being exceptionally good at one or the other "polarity" is not enough.

Mastery, then, requires a focus on all areas of an endeavor and the pursuit of excellence in each. The more you improve your skill in one area, the more it calls forth your developmental needs in the others. Whatever you neglect becomes your weak link.

This principle of mastery lies at the heart of taking a multi-dimensional approach to transformation. Mastery suggests that leaders and consultants must become conscious of and competent in *all* of the different dimensions of transformation, even those that they are not yet aware of or comfortable addressing—areas that are "outside the box."

Leading transformation *masterfully* requires that leaders and consultants attend to the dynamics within twenty-one different dimensions, all of which will be addressed in this book. Some of these dynamics are common and familiar. Many are not. Those that are familiar to most leaders and traditional management consultants pertain to *external* reality, as in organizational structures, systems, and business processes. Those that are most familiar to OD consultants pertain to *internal* reality, such as perception, feelings, interpersonal relationships, and culture. Mastery, of course, requires that leaders and consultants develop their awareness and skill in *both* arenas, internal and external.

The Three Elements of a Comprehensive Transformation Strategy

The three elements of a comprehensive transformation strategy speak directly to this need for a multi-dimensional approach. A comprehensive transformation strategy must include competent attention to (1) content, (2) people, and (3) process. *Content* refers to *what* about the organization needs to change, which are usually components found in the external domain, such as strategy, structure, systems, processes, technology, work practices, etc. *People* refers to the behaviors, emotions, minds, and spirits of the *human beings* who are designing, implementing, supporting, or being impacted by the change (mostly internal domains). *Process* refers to *how* the content and people changes will be planned for, designed, and implemented. In other words, process denotes the actions that will produce both the external (content) and internal (people) changes.

All three areas must be *integrated* into one unified transformation effort that moves an organization from where it is today to where it chooses to be in the future. Organizations that take a piecemeal approach and separate their organizational and technical changes (content) from their human and cultural changes (people) fail dramatically.

Separating *content* change and *people* change is common practice. This is one of the many reasons that leaders' track records at successful transformation are so poor. Generally speaking, the content advocates, such as those promoting reengineering, restructuring, and information technology applications, such as SAP implementation, and business strategy, do not understand human and cultural change (the interior domains). In the same way, most people proponents, such as human resource professionals, organization development practitioners, team builders, personal growth trainers, and executive coaches, do not understand pure organizational and technical changes (the exterior domains). Consequently, transformation is usually designed and run as separate, non-integrated initiatives. This just does not work. Focusing only on content, or fantasizing that organization transformation is only about people, or attending to both external and internal domains yet in an insufficient or non-integrated way are all equally effective paths to failure.

How can you integrate these often conflicting elements of the interior and exterior domains? By *consciously* designing your change process! Although change strategy requires attention to all three critical areas of content (what), people (who), and process (how), process is the integrating factor—the dimension that links and unites the exterior and interior domains. Consequently, transformation requires an integrated process approach.

Content change and people change will become integrated into one unified change effort only if you consciously design the process of transformation to perform that integration. Furthermore, the process of transformation, or how the change effort actually rolls out, will ultimately determine whether or not people buy into and commit to implementing the content of the transformation. If you design a poor process that alienates your people, the transformation will suffer—even if your content changes perfectly fit your organization's current needs. Process, ultimately, determines the success of your change implementation. Neglect process, or remain unconscious of the unique process dynamics and requirements of transformation, and you might as well neglect transformation, for it just won't happen. You must enter the arena of successful transformation through the process door.

This leads us to the main theme of this book: Leading transformation successfully requires that leaders and consultants focus on the dynamics of both human consciousness and change process.

An Invitation to Join the Exploration

Focusing on the dynamics of human consciousness and the transformational change process has been the backbone of our consulting and training practices for over twenty years. With all of our clients, we have attempted to take a conscious approach that blends attention to content, people, and process. Our consulting careers have been dedicated to understanding the multi-dimensionality of change, including how to change organizations as well as people. For years, we have attempted to integrate both the "hard" external and "soft" internal aspects of change, believing deeply that this integration was not only required, but represented the next evolution (beyond change management) that change leadership and consulting practices needed to embrace.

Building a multi-dimensional, process-oriented approach to transforming people and organizations has been our sole field of study. Our exploration continues and will certainly never be complete. In fact, the more we learn, the more we realize just how much we do not know. We write this book, therefore, not to share finite conclusions, but to reveal our latest insights. Our hope is that you will find the approach we offer to leading transformation compelling enough to join us in further exploring and developing it.

By nature, we are "action theorists." We read, study, and research, then rely heavily on our intuition to crystallize and integrate new learnings. We then build models and processes that we test heavily in the field with our clients. With their assistance, we next refine and evolve our thinking and practices. We attempt to be "pie-in-the-sky" visionaries, while remaining true and devoted pragmatists. We like our feet on the ground while our heads are in the stars.

We have engaged in this action research of conscious transformation for nearly two decades, yet our research base is rather small. Our small firm can serve only so many clients, especially given the fact that large system transformation efforts are long-term, often lasting three to five or more years. So, although we invite you into this action research with us, we must, in all conscience, admit that these theories and tools are not "proven" in their entirety. More people, both consultants and leaders, are needed to add to the research base for the approaches we describe here. We hope that you will test the ideas and practices presented in this book, then expand on them based on your own expertise and personal findings. With your participation, this action research can grow and become available to even more organizations undergoing transformation. We are confident that your reward will be well worth the risk of experimentation.

Our Audience

Over the years, we have been fortunate to work extensively with both change leaders and change consultants. Sometimes, our clients are the senior leaders of the organization; at other times, our clients are the internal change consultants supporting those leaders. Usually and ideally, our clients include both the senior leaders and their internal change consultants.

In this book, we will thoroughly explore transformation and will provide an overview of what we believe it takes to both *lead* transformation and *consult* to it successfully. Consequently, we write for *both* leaders and consultants.

Certainly, there is a school of thought that suggests that we ought to separate the leader and consultant audiences and write specifically for each. This notion is especially valid given the OD series of which this book is a part. However, we feel strongly that treating leaders and consultants separately and delivering individual messages, tools, and techniques to them has been part of the reason for failure in transformation.

Yes, leaders and consultants have unique roles that require specialized skills, but transformation demands a common understanding and skill set. This does not mean that the two roles (leading and consulting) should merge into one. Leaders must continue to lead, and consultants must continue to consult. Yet to be effective in transformation, leaders must develop people and process skills previously reserved for or shunted to their consulting counterparts, and consultants must become more grounded in core business skills and strategies previously reserved for leaders. We intend this book to assist both along their respective developmental paths to becoming more competent "change leaders."

Some of our discussions will clearly be geared to one or the other audience. At times, we will offer specific insights and techniques for leaders and at other times present specific consulting approaches and tools. However, in all cases, the "secondary" audience will benefit greatly from the discussion and from fully exploring the information and insights offered.

Given our bias and intent, we use the labels "leader" and "change leader" to refer to both leaders and consultants. When we refer solely to one or the other, we will make that clear.

We write with leaders of all levels in mind, with the key focus on leaders who have responsibility for designing, influencing, or implementing their organization's transformational change plans. This obviously includes CEOs and other senior executives, but also mid-managers, supervisors, and employees who play vital roles on change project teams.

The change consultants who will receive the most value from this book are those responsible for educating, advising, and coaching line leaders to develop and implement large-scale transformational change strategy. Such consultants definitely include *process consultants*, such as organization development practitioners, change management specialists, and process improvement facilitators. It also includes all *content consultants*, especially those with expertise in creating e-commerce businesses within existing organizations, business process reengineering, information technology, knowledge management systems, business strategy, organizational redesign and restructuring, manufacturing technology and systems, and human resources.

We believe that this book will have broad appeal to anyone interested in or impacted by transformation. Consequently, we also write for educators and students of change. Educators can include vice presidents of human resources, management development trainers, college and business school professors, public school administrators, executive coaches, and public speakers. Students of change can literally be anyone, whether enrolled in school, working in the public or private sectors, or simply lay people seeking to further understand one core dynamic of the 21st Century—transformation!

And last, we write this book for all the targets of change, those people who are directly impacted by the quantity and quality of change that is rolling through all of our lives. For these people, who may not be able to influence directly *how* their organization's transformation is occurring, we offer this material as support, knowing that anyone equipped with a better understanding of the dynamics of transformation will be better able to cope with it and thrive through its implementation.

A Larger Body of Work

The structure of the book is designed as part of a larger body of work that includes a companion book, *The Change Leader's Roadmap: How to Navigate Your Organization's Transformation,* also in this OD series, and a complete set of change tools, published by Being First, Inc., our training and consulting firm.

Either book can stand alone, that is, one does not need to read the other in order to get value from them. However, the two books were written simultaneously and thus provide a complete overview of conscious transformation.

This book describes the *conceptual overview* of conscious transformation and what it requires to lead it successfully, whereas *The Change Leader's Roadmap* provides a thorough description of the actual Change Process Methodology that puts these concepts into *practice.* In other words, this book provides the theoretical foundation, and *The Change Leader's Roadmap* provides pragmatic guidance and tools. We have written both because of our devotion to blending concept and technique. (One without the other always falls short.) Given our bias for blending theory with pragmatic approaches, we offer tools and worksheets where appropriate throughout this book. And *The Change Leader's Roadmap* connects its pragmatic guidance directly back to the theoretical basis offered here. The change tools published by Being First are more comprehensive and detailed than what is offered in either book.

Our desire in writing these two books and in publishing the change tools is to provide all the support we can for your application of this conscious, multi-dimensional, process-oriented approach to leading and consulting to organization transformation.

Structure of This Book

There are four sections to this book. Section One, "A Call for Conscious Transformation," contains three chapters. In Chapter One, "The Drivers of Change," we address what is catalyzing change in today's organizations and, specifically, what is catalyzing transformational change. We demonstrate how transformation includes more drivers than other types of change, making it more complex and challenging. In Chapter Two, "Three Types of Organization Change," we define transformation and contrast it with the two other types of change that leaders face.

In Chapter Three, "Two Leadership Approaches to Transformation," we describe two very different approaches that leaders and consultants bring to transformation and the impact each has on their on potential success. In this discussion, we clarify why transformation requires leaders and consultants to become more conscious in their approach.

In Section Two, "Mindset: The Leverage Point for Transformation," we focus directly on the essential human dynamics of change. Specifically, in Chapter Four, "The Role and Impact of Mindset," we define mindset and demonstrate how it influences what change leaders perceive in their transformations and the results they are able to produce. We also discuss why self-management and personal transformation are required competencies in both leaders and consultants. In Chapter Five, "Fundamental Assumptions About Reality," we explore mindset more deeply, looking into the fundamental assumptions about reality, organizations, and change that leaders and consultants currently hold. We explore how these deep-rooted beliefs must transform to enable leaders and consultants to succeed at transforming organizations. Specifically, we explore the Emerging Mindset that carries the hope of producing more successful transformation efforts and outline the ten operating principles for conscious transformation that come directly from it and their impact on change leadership.

In Section Three, "A Process Orientation for Leading Transformation," we present a greatly expanded view of the process dynamics inherent in transformation. In Chapter Six, "Conscious Process Thinking," we demonstrate that leaders' traditional "project thinking" mentality prevents transformation and show how systems thinking is a move in the right direction, albeit one leaders have not taken far enough. We introduce conscious process thinking and overview three very different change leadership styles, suggesting that a "facilitative" style has the greatest probability for success with today's leaders. In Chapter Seven, "Change Process Models," we introduce change process models, contrast them to change frameworks, and describe why change frameworks don't suffice for guiding transformation. We also introduce the nine-phase Change Process Model for Facilitating Conscious Transformation and the concept of "thinking disciplines" as a replacement for "checklists of prescribed action," which are not applicable to the realities of transformation.

Section Four, "Conscious Transformational Leadership," consists of two chapters that discuss the implications for leaders and consultants seeking to become conscious transformational leaders. In Chapter Eight, "Developing Conscious

Change Leaders," we describe how the role of leadership has evolved and what is required to create a comprehensive development curriculum for building an organization's change leadership capacity. We include an overview of the knowledge areas, behaviors, and ways of being most suited to conscious transformational leaders. We close with Chapter Nine, "The Leadership Choice to Transform," which provides guidance for developing your individual capacity to embrace and succeed in leading transformation consciously.

In writing this book, we aspire to communicate what is possible in leading conscious transformation. We dream a dream here, a dream that has transformation actually deliver its intended business results and more. We dream of transformation that has positive impacts beyond profitability and shareholder value. We dream of transformation that improves people's lives, deepens their ability to get what they want, and strengthens their relationships, trust, and joy in working together for common goals and aspirations. We dream of transformation that positively contributes to communities, societies, and nations. We dream of transformation that is so user-friendly that it bolsters people's resolve and capacity for even more positive change in themselves and the world.

Nothing would give us greater satisfaction than to know that this book has added to the possibilities of these dreams. We hope it serves you well.

Section One
A Call for Conscious Transformation

Chapter 1: The Drivers of Change

Chapter 2: Three Types of Organization Change

Chapter 3: Two Leadership Approaches to Transformation

1

The Drivers of Change

ORGANIZATION CHANGE DOESN'T HAPPEN OUT OF THE BLUE.
It is catalyzed by a number of forces that trigger first awareness and then action.
These signals for change usually originate in the organization's environment or
marketplace. Such signals can include bold moves by competitors, new technology, or shifts in government regulations. Failures in the performance of a leader's
own organization can also signal the need for change. Whatever their source,
these events require the organization to respond.

Too often signals for change occur without leaders noticing. Or leaders may
receive a signal for change and act on it without fully understanding its implications, or worse, without appreciating what change in the organization the signal is
requiring. These shortcomings limit leaders' ability to define the change needed
and the outcomes for it. How do leaders explore these signals and accurately interpret their meaning? How can they be more certain that they are asking their organizations to change in the ways that are really needed?

It is our experience that leaders are becoming much more attuned to reading
the trends in their changing environments and, from this, creating new business

strategies to respond more appropriately to them. They are making great strides in changing how their organizations are structured and run to fulfill these new business strategies. However, it is also our experience that most leaders are not carrying their required changes far enough. They lack understanding of the scope of change that is required to get the business outcomes they need.

It is critical for leaders to understand what drives change. It is essential that leaders comprehend the entire breadth of today's drivers for change and be able to respond to each of them appropriately, not just for today, but for the organization's future success.

The Drivers of Change

The Drivers of Change Model (see Figure 1.1) clarifies what drives the need for change, especially transformational change. The model portrays a sequence to these triggers, with one trigger calling forth change in the next, and the next, and so on. A demand-and-response relationship exists between these various catalysts, although many of the forces are in fact iterative and can have reciprocal influence. The linear sequence shown in the figure, however, is critical to understanding the complexity of change that leaders face today.

The model describes seven drivers, four that leaders are most familiar with and three that are relatively new to their leadership screens. It shows that the drivers move from what is *external* and impersonal (environment, marketplace, organizations) to what is *internal* and personal (culture and people).

The Drivers of Change Model illustrates that changes in the larger external domains, such as shifts in the environment or marketplace, demand a response (change) in the more specific domains of business strategy and organizational design, which, in turn, require change in the human domains of culture and people's behaviors and ways of thinking. The external domains are clearly more familiar to leaders—environment, marketplace, business, and organization—while the internal ones—culture, behavior, and mindset—are new to most, yet equally essential. If leaders do not attend to the internal domains and adapt them to the forces of change exerted by the external domains, then their change efforts fail.

Many of the current struggles with transformation are a result of leaders not attending to the cultural, behavioral, and mindset components of transformation or not attending to them in ways that make a real impact. We will provide guidelines for leaders in how to address the more person-focused drivers of change while *simultaneously* meeting the needs of the external drivers. Of course, it is equally true that attending only to the internal drivers and neglecting the external ones will also cause

Figure 1.1.   The Drivers of Change Model

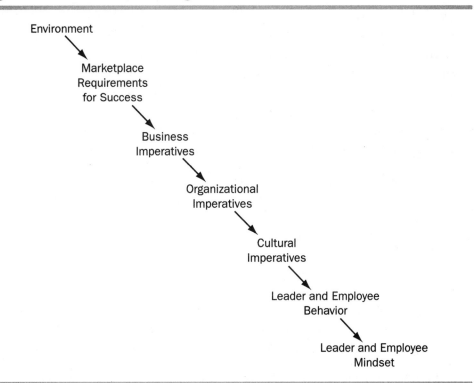

transformation to fail. The point is that both the external *and* the internal drivers must be included in the scope of the change. Let's define the terms in the Drivers of Change Model and then explore the message the model delivers.

Environment.   The dynamics of the larger context within which organizations and people operate. These forces include:

- Social,
- Business and economic,
- Political,
- Governmental,
- Technological,
- Demographic,
- Legal, and
- Natural environment.

Marketplace Requirements for Success. The aggregate set of customer requirements that determine what it takes for a business to succeed in its marketplace and meet its customers' needs. This includes not only actual product or service needs, but also requirements such as speed of delivery, customization capability, level of quality, need for innovation, level of customer service, and so forth. Changes in marketplace requirements are the result of changes in environmental forces. For instance, as the environment is becoming infused with technology that makes speed and innovation commonplace, customers are demanding higher quality, customized products and services and expecting them faster.

Business Imperatives. Business imperatives outline what the company must do *strategically* to be successful, given its customers' changing requirements. These can require systematic rethinking and change to the company's mission, strategy, goals, business model, products, services, pricing, or branding. Essentially, business imperatives pertain to the organization's *strategy* for successfully meeting its customer requirements.

Organizational Imperatives. Organizational imperatives specify what must change in the organization's structure, systems, processes, technology, resources, skill base, or staffing to implement and achieve its strategic business imperatives successfully.

Cultural Imperatives. Cultural imperatives denote how the norms, or collective way of being, working, and relating in the company, must change to support and drive the organization's new design, operations, and strategy. For instance, a culture of teamwork may be required to support reengineering business processes (organizational imperatives) to drive the strategy (business imperative) of faster cycle time and increased customer responsiveness.

Leader and Employee Behavior. Collective behavior creates and expresses an organization's culture. Behavior speaks to more than just overt actions: It describes the style, tone, or character that permeates what people do. It speaks to how people's way of being must change to establish a new culture. Therefore, leader and employee behavior denotes the ways in which leaders and employees must behave differently to re-create the organization's culture to implement and sustain the new organizational design successfully.

Leader and Employee Mindset. Mindset encompasses the worldview, assumptions, beliefs, or mental models that cause people to behave and act as they do. Becoming aware that each of us has a mindset, and that it directly impacts our behavior, decisions, actions, and results, is often the critical first step in building a person's and an organization's capacity to transform. Marilyn Ferguson, in *The Aquarian Conspiracy* (1987), states, "If you continue to think as you have always thought, you will continue to get what you have always gotten." Transforming mindset is a prerequisite to sustained change in behavior and culture. A shift of mindset is often required for organizational leaders to recognize changes in the environmental forces and marketplace requirements, thereby being able to determine the best new strategic business direction, structure, or operation for the organization. A change in employee mindset is often required for them to understand the rationale for the changes being asked of them. And almost always, leaders and employees must change their mindset to implement and function in the organization's new design and strategy successfully.

When the scope of change in the environment and marketplace is minimal, content change usually suffices. When change is required only to business and organizational imperatives (content) and not to culture, behavior, or mindset (people), the type of change is developmental or transitional. (The different types of change will be described in detail in the next chapter.) However, when the magnitude of environmental or marketplace change is large, then it triggers the need for *radical* content change, which drives the need for change in culture and people. This type of change, which includes all these drivers, is transformational. By definition, transformational change requires that leaders attend to content (external, impersonal) as well as people (internal, personal).

▶ CASE ɪɴ POINT

A brief review of the divestiture of the Bell Operating Companies from AT&T provides a great illustration of the Drivers of Change Model in action. We use this example because it is so widely known and effectively demonstrates how the Drivers of Change work. Jesse L. Brooks, III, and Heddy Peña were with AT&T for twenty years before and during the breakup. Providing an overview, they write:

> "Pre-divestiture, the old 'Ma Bell' was a company of one million plus employees and the largest employer in the private sector. Its ubiquitous presence and its paternalistic/maternalistic culture earned the company its nickname of 'Ma Bell.' As the name indicates, the company 'took care' of its employees. Given its monopoly status, it had the luxury of doing so. Employment was typically 'for life,' and jobs were never high pressure.

"AT&T's monopoly status gave the company a certain profit that was guaranteed by the government. In 1984, the government pursued the break-up of AT&T, resulting in it keeping its long distance business, while the local service businesses went to the regional Bell Operating Companies."

Here is an illustration of how the Drivers of Change Model manifested at AT&T. Notice how the forces in the external domains called forth and required the changes in the internal domains. Also notice how the massive "content" changes could not have been implemented or sustained without significant transformation to the organization's culture and the behavior and mindset of the leaders and employees.

Environmental Forces

·   *Government Regulations:* FCC forced AT&T to form a fully separate utility (first American Bell, then AT&T Information Systems); anti-trust laws created an even playing field for domestic competition.

·   *Changes in Technology:* Expansion of microwave technology and capability; first commercial communications satellite, Telstar 1, in orbit; introduction of electronic components into customer premises and network equipment; computers blurring the distinction between voice and data transmission and between data transmission and data processing.

·   *Customers:* Increased competition allowed by the FCC.

Marketplace Requirements for Success

·   Focus on the customer;

·   Customers demanded technology that directly served their needs;

·   Customization of communication solutions;

·   Demand for high-speed transmission;

·   Demand for higher quality of service and equipment; and

·   Demand for lower costs, despite Bell's continued tariffs.

Business Imperatives

·   Become more competitive and customer focused;

·   Lower bottom-line operating costs and improve profitability;

- Tailor equipment and service to customer needs;

- Lower price of service;

- Acquire new companies to expand services (McGaw for wireless; NCR for computers); and

- Shift focus of Bell Laboratories from winning new patents to producing sellable customer products.

Organizational Imperatives

- Downsize to enable lower cost structure;

- Build a strong marketing organization that includes a new sales force and product development functions;

- Shift from blue collar to white collar job focus (high tech, sales and marketing) and develop appropriate skills;

- Restructure company into strategic business units along product lines to reflect the needs of the marketplace; and

- Streamline processes to increase efficiency and cost savings.

Cultural Imperatives

- Shift from family culture to bottom-line orientation;

- Shift from being internally focused to being market and customer focused;

- Shift from communal to competitive orientation;

- Shift from entitlement to empowerment; and

- Shift from laissez-faire to accountability.

Leadership and Employee Behavior

- Focus on results, not just activities;

- Share information and communicate openly;

- Take risks;

- Become more entrepreneurial and innovative;

- Act more quickly and decisively in new marketing environment;

- Become more accountable to Wall Street; and

- Become more collaborative and less autocratic.

Leadership and Employee Mindset

- Leaders:

  Shift mindset from "the customer doesn't matter" to "the customer is primary";

  Shift focus from "study and document" to "act and learn";

  Think like an entrepreneur;

  Shift from a "take it or leave it" attitude toward customers to become more image, brand, and service conscious; and

  Shift from command and control style toward coaching and motivating.

- Employees:

  Shift from "job for life" to "earn my way" through my results and contribution;

  Shift from "family" atmosphere to "look after myself";

  Shift from "do as your supervisor tells you" to "be empowered to do the job as you see it!";

  Shift from "cover your arse" to being accountable; and

  Shift from avoiding failure to learning through prudent risk taking. ◀

Exhibit 1.1 offers a worksheet to assist your assessment of the actual drivers at play in your organization. Fill it out, carefully thinking through each point, and then discuss your conclusions with others to obtain the most benefit.

The Evolution of Change and the Required Expansion of Leadership Awareness and Attention

Over the past forty years, the nature of organization change has evolved tremendously, increasing the areas of organizational life to which leaders must attend. The Drivers of Change Model both predicts and describes this evolution and the subsequent increase in leadership awareness required.

Exhibit 1.1. What Is Driving Your Organization's Change?

Environmental Forces:

Marketplace Requirements for Success:

Business Imperatives:

Organizational Imperatives:

Cultural Imperatives:

Leader and Employee Behavior:

    Leaders:

    Employees:

Leader and Employee Mindset:

    Leaders:

    Employees:

The History of Organization Change

Before the 1970s, leaders as a whole paid relatively little attention to their external environment, including their customers, competitors, or the marketplace in general. If they had market share, that was all that mattered. Then, during the 1970s, technology, innovation, and deregulation (environmental forces) began to shake up many industries, including automobile, steel, manufacturing, communications, banking, and retail. These environmental forces began to alter the marketplace requirements for success in these industries. As leaders struggled to differentiate their organizations' strategic advantages, strategy development (business imperatives) became the leadership rave. Led by a few large consulting firms, many of the Fortune 500 began to review and evolve their business strategy systematically and seek to comprehend their business imperatives. As a result, an increase in new products and services was seen during this time.

In the late 1970s, the scope of change increased, further causing leaders' focus to turn to the organization and how to improve it (organizational imperatives). Productivity improvement, restructuring, downsizing, work redesign, quality, and process improvement swept the country. This focus on organizational improvement intensified in the mid-1980s with the quality movement, then again in the early 1990s with the reengineering craze, and continues today with the information technology movement, enterprise resource planning efforts, and the search for how to master global connectivity via the World Wide Web.

Up to this point, most change efforts focused on external drivers. For the most part, these content changes were *relatively* comfortable for most leaders. Why? Because most of today's leaders come from engineering, financial, military, or legal backgrounds. For them, altering the strategy, structure, systems, processes, and technology of the great organizational "machine" is familiar territory. It is tangible, observable, and measurable. And, most importantly, it carries the illusion of control.

Truth be told, many of these "content" changes *could* be tightly managed. Leaders could command and control many of them to their desired outcomes. This was possible for two reasons. First, leaders could often design and implement changes as separate initiatives, requiring little integration and no special attention to process. Leaders could simply manage these projects using the project management skills and tools they had honed over the years. Second, these changes usually did not require any significant or profound personal change on the part of the leaders or the people impacted by the change. A bit more communication and training in the new systems were usually enough to handle the "people" aspects of these "content" changes.

The "change is manageable" bubble began to burst in the mid-1980s, and by the 1990s it became glaringly obvious that truly managing change was becoming less and less possible. The technological revolution, primarily fueled by information and communication technology, had increased the speed and scope of change so much that the process of change became significantly more complex. Isolated and distinct change initiatives no longer sufficed as organization change became more and more enterprise-wide. Leading change now demanded the integration of numerous cross-functional initiatives, and leaders' traditional, project management techniques did not provide adequately for complex process integration. New, more evolved approaches were required.

Furthermore, the tangible domain of changing organizational strategy, structure, systems, processes, skills, and technology suddenly required a significant focus on the less tangible domain of culture and people (cultural imperatives). This new requirement for attention to people was captured in an article in *The Wall Street Journal* on November 26, 1996. It stated, "Gurus of the $4.7 billion reengineering industry like [Michael] Hammer forgot about people. 'I wasn't smart enough about that,' Hammer commented. 'I was reflecting my engineering background and was insufficiently appreciative of the human dimension. I've learned that's critical.'" Suddenly, change was significantly less manageable and required more attention to people and process than leaders were equipped to give.

Although the change management field had begun in the early 1980s through the work of thought leaders such as Linda Ackerman and Daryl Conner, it was in the mid-1990s that change management began to be seen as absolutely necessary. Overnight, the major "content" change consulting firms began change management practices. However, these early mass-marketed approaches only scratched the surface of the attention to people and process needed. For the most part, they addressed only the complaints surfaced by dissatisfied leaders—how to improve communications, overcome employee resistance, and manage implementation better. Even in these symptomatic areas, the approaches offered were mostly insufficient, as the content consulting firms did not really understand the internal dynamics of people and culture, nor how to design change processes that integrated basic human needs. Most of these early approaches made the mistake of applying change "management" techniques to people and process dynamics that were inherently unmanageable.

A major source of the failure of most of the change efforts of the past decade has been the lack of leader and consultant skill in the internal domain of people. Let's continue to explore the historical chronology, using the remaining Drivers of

Change to demonstrate how profoundly people have been drawn into the change equation in recent years.

Starting in the mid-1980s, the marketplace forces were requiring such significant content change that an organization's people and culture also needed to change in order to implement and sustain the content changes successfully. Culture change was no longer a "nice to do"; it was now beginning to be recognized as a "must do," as noted in Michael Hammer's comment.

The earlier case example of the breakup of AT&T is a great illustration of how the scope of environmental and marketplace-driven change grew from business and organizational imperatives to include cultural imperatives, behavior, and mindset. After the breakup, AT&T required not just a new business strategy, but also a complete overhaul of its organizational structure, systems, processes, and skill base. Yet, none of this could have succeeded without the simultaneous transformation of its entitlement culture, to which AT&T devoted significant resources.

When change in the business and organizational imperatives is relatively small, leaders can ignore culture, because the existing culture simply absorbs the incremental changes. But when the change to the strategy, structure, systems, processes, or technology is significant, and requires a new way of being, working, or relating in order to operate the new organization, then leaders are required to change cultural norms for the change to succeed. With this requirement of leaders to attend to culture and people, organizational change now entered the realm of transformation.

Not surprisingly, in the early 1980s the Organization Transformation movement, which focused heavily on cultural change, was born. Some factions of the organization development profession embraced and explored this new field enthusiastically. Leaders, however, did not take this movement seriously until more recently. The reasons why are inherent in the remaining two Drivers of Change.

In order to change culture, or the collective norm of how people behave, individuals must change their behavior (leader and employee behavior). If the individual behavior change that is required is minimal and simply entails skill improvement or minor adjustment to work practices, then basic skill training or slight behavior modification is all that is required. (Deep personal reflection and self-development can be ignored.) However, when the required behavior and style change are significant, as in most of today's transformations, then people's mindsets must also change (leader and employee mindset). If people do not alter the worldview or beliefs that drive their current behavior, then they cannot sustain major behavioral change.

Let us underscore that change in behavior and mindset is required by *both* leaders and employees. For example, in the AT&T case, both leaders and employees had to engage in more accountable work practices, which required both to alter their mindsets. Both needed to embrace the new world of competition mentally and emotionally in order to really believe that they had to be more accountable. Leaders and employees had to change their fundamental worldview of what was required of them to succeed. They had to embrace the idea that they were not *entitled* to success, but must *earn* it through their performance, individually and collectively. Once this new mindset was adopted, more accountable work practices came more easily to both leaders and employees.

Ideally, leaders and employees must change their behavior and mindset *simultaneously* because key aspects of culture are largely the product of interactive behavior patterns between leaders and employees and the underlying mindsets that drive these behaviors. For culture to change, these patterns must break, which requires change on both sides of the equation. At AT&T, for example, the cultural shift from entitlement to empowerment required leaders to step out of their command and control style while employees stepped into greater self-reliance and responsibility. A shift on only one side of the equation creates conflict; a shift on both sides creates sustainable change.

By the early 1990s, the scope and required focus of organization change had fully evolved and entered the unpredictable and uncertain world of human beings. It is no wonder that empowerment, self-management, emotional intelligence, personal mastery, and learning have become topics of interest over the past ten years. In the 21st Century, however, these must become more than simply points of interest, experiments, or topics of casual conversation; leaders and consultants must actually *use* them to produce tangible transformation. *In today's business environment, significant transformation cannot happen without the simultaneous transformation of a critical mass of leaders' and employees' mindsets and behavior. Conscious transformation means attending to the consciousness of the people in your organization, including your own.*

Leaders and consultants who place personal mindset change for both themselves and employees at the center of their organizations' transformations will succeed. Those who refuse to acknowledge this need will fail. The bad news is that most leaders and consultants, up to now, have denied this need. The good news is that more and more leaders and consultants are beginning to embrace this fundamental requirement of organizational transformation.

► CASE ɪɴ POINT

In the late 1980s, we worked with a large bank in California and ran smack into this leadership denial factor. This was during the time that the "change is manageable" bubble was just beginning to burst, and most leaders were unaware of the deep personal change being required both for themselves and for employees.

The bank was installing a new computer system throughout its many branches that would revolutionize their tellers' jobs by putting substantial customer information at their fingertips. Equipped with this information, tellers would then be expected by management to introduce and sell appropriate insurance and investment products to their customers while the customers were at the tellers' windows making deposits or withdrawals. The technology installation was part of a comprehensive strategy to expand the bank's service offerings to retain customers and market share, which the bank was quickly losing to large investment brokerages.

Senior management asked us to audit their existing change strategy and to predict how we thought it would proceed. After interviews with senior executives, we realized that they clearly understood that their marketplace had new requirements for success and that they had developed a solid business strategy based on new business imperatives. They had effectively translated that strategy into new organizational imperatives, primarily the installation of new computer technology. However, that was as far as they had gone. They conceived the change as a simple technology installation. But it was much, much more.

The senior leaders had no idea that their new marketplace requirements and business and organizational imperatives were so significant that they were driving the need for a fundamental transformation of their culture, as well as their leaders' and employees' skills, behaviors, and mindsets. Their change strategy neglected any attention to culture, behavior, and mindset beyond training the tellers in how to use the new computer system. To the leaders, that was enough. They planned to shut all of their numerous branches down on a Friday, work all through the weekend installing the system and training employees, and re-open the bank on Monday morning without skipping a beat. They were in for a painful surprise.

We issued a loud warning that their plan was going to backfire and cause tremendous upheaval because their strategy neglected any attention to changing their culture or their leaders' and employees' behavior and mindset. We suggested that, in the best-case scenario, their change effort would alienate employees and customers; in the worst case, it would cause both to leave in droves.

Here were the key issues as we saw them:

1. Each branch was a fiefdom, run top-down by largely autocratic branch managers who made all significant customer decisions. We suggested that the new technology and the subsequent change in the tellers' role would create a power struggle between the branch managers and the tellers. The fact that the tellers would now have the power to make significant customer decisions would undermine the branch managers' historic authority, and the branch managers would be likely to withhold their support, which the tellers would so desperately need, especially during the initial stages of implementation.

2. Many of the tellers had worked for the bank for ten or more years and were hired because of their style and skill at doing accurate and predictable work, that is, helping customers to make deposits and withdrawals. The tellers had no sales training. Most, if not all, were not salespeople by nature, and their communications skills were not highly sophisticated. They took jobs at the bank because they were attracted to the safe and predictable work of making customer transactions.

3. We suggested that employees would learn the new system (they were all good "soldiers") but not be willing to use it because to do so would be too threatening to them. Not possessing the mindset, behavior, or skills of a salesperson, they would simply not engage their customers in the new sales-oriented conversation that their leaders expected. And, if they did attempt such conversations, their lack of skill might backfire, creating resentment or embarrassment for customers and reducing customer satisfaction.

4. Management planned to change the tellers' compensation system to drive their new behavior. A significant portion of their compensation was to be based on hitting sales targets. We suggested that installing this new compensation system at startup, before the change was assimilated, would alienate the tellers and that this

resentment would further amplify the weakness in their sales skills. We also suggested that the new compensation system would increase the conflict between the tellers and their angry branch managers because the branch managers would pressure or punish the tellers for not hitting their "sales" numbers.

The unfortunate conclusion to this story was that the leaders rejected our concerns and proceeded with their original plan. Given their mindset and lack of desire to address any potential problems, they simply did not want to hear what we had to say about the need to attend to culture, behavior, and mindset as a part of their overall change strategy. The outcome of their change was as we predicted. Over the next eighteen months, the bank lost both market share and many of its top employees, including *both* tellers and branch managers. ◀

The point is this: Like it or not, most of the significant changes in organizations today require leaders to attend to culture, behavior, and mindset, including their own. A major focus of change consultants has to be helping leaders in this endeavor. Leaders and consultants must understand at which point they must integrate personal change into organization change and how to accomplish it, for if they do not, they will fail.

Summary

Prior to the 1980s, leaders could limit the scope of their change efforts to business strategy and the redesign of their organizations and be successful. But that's no longer the case—not today and not tomorrow. Every year, as the demands of the environment increase at astronomical rates, people are forced to change their behavior and mindsets to keep pace. Traditional change management practices are insufficient. The next evolution of change leadership is already here, requiring the integration of organization and personal change into one unified effort. This is a key success factor in leading transformational change. Chapter Two explores this point further by clarifying the unique requirements of transformational change as contrasted to the other types of change occurring in organizations today.

Three Types of
Organization Change

THE INUIT PEOPLE HAVE TWENTY different words to describe "snow," all referring to the same cold, white stuff. When you are as familiar with something as the Inuit people are with winter weather, you recognize subtle differences and distinctions that the rest of us don't. These distinctions enable the Inuit people to deal appropriately with the weather. They have clothes and snowshoes designed for wet snow and clothes and snowshoes designed for dry snow. So it is with change; leaders must know the type of change they face before they can know how to lead it.

Before the 1980s, the term "change" described everything that needed to be different in organizations. However, as change proliferated and we had more experience with it in our consulting, we began to notice differences in the changes our clients faced. Linda Ackerman Anderson (1986), in an article in the *Organization Development Practitioner*, defined the three most prevalent types of change occurring in organizations as *developmental change, transitional change,* and *transformational change.* At that time, it had become painfully apparent that consultants and executives alike needed to understand and differentiate the types of change they were attempting to manage in their organizations. One size did not fit all. As with snow, knowing the type of change you are dealing with is paramount to building an effective strategy to deal with it, as each type of change requires a different approach.

In this chapter, we build on Ackerman Anderson's original work, describing each type of change, providing examples, and discussing similarities and differences, especially as they relate to culture, people, and process. Additionally, we include some of the implications that each type of change has for change leadership and for change strategy. Figure 2.1 graphically shows the three types of change. Table 2.1 compares them across a range of relevant factors.

Figure 2.1. Three Types of Organization Change

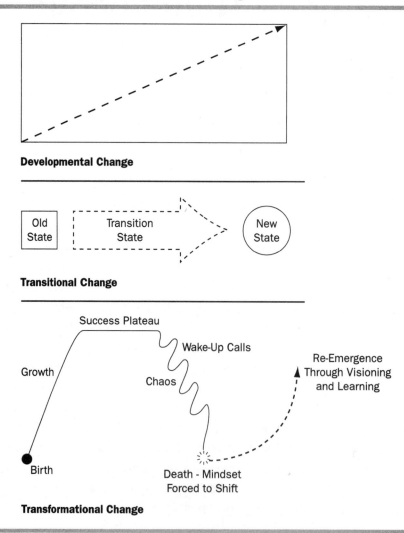

Developmental Change

Transitional Change

Transformational Change

Table 2.1. Matrix of the Three Types of Organization Change

Type	Degree of Pain Felt	Primary Motivation	Degree of Threat to Survival	Gap Between Environmental Needs & Operations	Clarity of Outcome	Impact on Mindset	Focus of Change	Orientation	Level of Personal Development Required	How Change Occurs
Developmental Change	1	Improvement	1	1	4 It is prescribed against a standard	1 Little if any	Improvement of skills, knowledge, practice, and performance	To do better in a certain area: project-oriented	1	Through training, skill development, communications, process improvement
Transitional Change	2	Fix a problem	2	2	4 It is designed against a criteria	1 Little if any	Redesign of strategy, structures, systems, processes, technology or work practices (not culture)	Project-oriented; largely focused on structure, technology, and work practices	2	Controlled process, support structures, timeline
Transformational Change	3-4	Survival: change or die; or Thrival: breakthrough needed to pursue new opportunities	1-4	3-4	1 It is not initially known; it emerges or is created through trial and error and continuous course correction	2-4 Forced to shift: old mindset and/or business paradigm must change	Overhaul of strategy, structure, systems processes, technology, work, culture, behavior, and mindset	Process-oriented requires shift in mindset, behavior, and culture	3-4	Conscious process design and facilitation; high involvement; emergent process

Rating Scale: 1 is low, 4 is high

Developmental Change

Look again at the developmental change model in Figure 2.1. As shown in Table 2.1, developmental change represents the *improvement* of an existing skill, method, performance standard, or condition that for some reason does not measure up to current or future needs. Metaphorically, developmental changes are improvements "within the box" of what is already known or practiced. Such improvements are often logical adjustments to current operations. They are motivated by the goal to do "better than" or do "more of" what is currently done. The key focus is to strengthen or correct what already exists in the organization, thus ensuring improved performance, continuity, and greater satisfaction. The process of development keeps people vibrant, growing, and stretching through the challenge of attaining new performance levels.

Developmental change is the simplest of the three types of change. In it, the new state is a prescribed enhancement of the old state, rather than a radical or experimental solution requiring profound change. Developmental change is usually a response to relatively small shifts in the environment or marketplace requirements for success—or simply the result of a continuous need to improve current operations (process improvement). The degree of pain triggering developmental change is usually low, at least in comparison to the other types of change. This does not mean that developmental change is not important or challenging; it is. However, the risks associated with developmental change, and the number of unpredictable and volatile variables tied to it, are considerably fewer than with the other two types of change.

In developmental change, the gap between what the environment or marketplace calls for and what currently exists is comparatively low. Consequently, the threat to the survival of the organization is also low. This makes creating and communicating a clear case for developmental change a far simpler matter than with the other two types of change.

Leaders can best initiate developmental change through sharing information about why the performance bar has to be raised and by setting stretch goals. When leaders challenge people to excel and provide them the resources and support to do so, this usually produces the necessary motivation for successful developmental change.

There are two primary assumptions in developmental change. First, people are capable of improving, and second, they will improve if provided the appropriate reasons, resources, motivation, and training.

The most commonly used developmental change strategy is training—in new skills, better communication, or new techniques or processes for accomplishing the higher goals. Leaders can use an assessment and problem-solving approach to identify, remove, or resolve what has blocked better performance. They can also use the existing goal-setting and reward systems to improve motivation and behavior.

Developmental change applies to individuals, groups, or the whole organization and is the primary type of change inherent in all of the following improvement processes:

- Training (both technical and personal), such as communications, interpersonal relations, and supervisory skills;

- Some applications of process improvement or quality;

- Some interventions for increasing cycle time;

- Team building;

- Problem solving;

- Improving communication;

- Conflict resolution;

- Increasing sales or production;

- Meeting management;

- Role negotiation;

- Survey feedback efforts;

- Job enrichment; and

- Expanding existing market outreach.

Transitional Change

As shown in Figure 2.1, transitional change is more complex. It is the required response to more significant shifts in environmental forces or marketplace requirements for success. Rather than simply improve *what is,* transitional change *replaces what is with something entirely different.*

Transitional change begins when leaders recognize that a problem exists or that an opportunity is not being pursued—and that something in the existing operation needs to change or be created to better serve current and/or future demands. Once executives, change leaders, or employee teams have assessed the needs and opportunities at hand, they design a more desirable future state to satisfy their distinct requirements. As can be seen from Figure 2.1, to achieve this new state, the organization must dismantle and emotionally let go of the old way of operating and move through a transition while the new state is being put into place.

Examples of Transitional Change

- Reorganizations;

- Simple mergers or consolidations;

- Divestitures;

- Installation and integration of computers or new technology that do not require major changes in mindset or behavior; and

- Creation of new products, services, systems, processes, policies, or procedures that replace old ones.

Richard Beckhard and Rubin Harris (1987) first named and defined transitional change in their Three States of Change model, which differentiated "old state," "new state," and "transition state." They articulated that transitional change requires the dismantling of the old state and the creation of a clearly designed new state, usually achieved over a set period of time, called the transition state. This state is unique and distinct from how the old state used to function or how the new state will function once in place. Beckhard and Harris were the first to suggest that changes of this nature could and needed to be *managed.* These two pioneers in the field of change management provided some critical strategies that continue to be useful today for transitional change.

Leaders typically perceive transitional changes as projects that can be managed against a budget and timeline, and rightfully so. Transitional changes usually have a specific start date and end date, as well as a known concrete outcome designed according to a set of preconceived design requirements. Traditional approaches to project management are usually quite effective for overseeing transitional change, especially when the people impacted by the change are fully aware of what is going on and are committed to making it happen. Project management approaches work best when there are few people issues because significant human variables usually make a project "unmanageable."

The degree of focus required for the human and cultural components is a key differentiator between transitional and transformational change. In transformational change, human and cultural issues are key drivers. In transitional change, they are often present, but are not dominant. For instance, in technology installations that are transitional in nature, such as simple software upgrades, the only behavioral change required is learning the new system. The new technology does not change people's roles, responsibilities, or decision-making authority. It merely improves how they do their current jobs. In technology changes that are transformational, such as in significant information technology installations, the new technology requires people's behavior, jobs, and perspectives on their lives or work to change, making the human impact and the change strategy required to deal with it much more complex.

It must be noted that William Bridges' work on transitions (Bridges, 1980; Bridges, 1991) is different from the transitional change to which we refer. Bridges' work focuses on understanding how people go through change psychologically and emotionally and on how to assist people to proceed through their personal process in effective and caring ways. Bridges' work is essential to appreciate and apply in all types of change in organizations, including transitional change from an old to a new state. All organizational change, regardless of the type, impacts people. The variable that affects change strategy is the degree and depth of the impact.

In transitional change, the requirements for deep personal change are low and quite predictable, making the human dynamics more "manageable" than in transformational change. Building a transitional change strategy and well-planned change process assists with the human requirement. If leaders experience difficult human and cultural impacts in transitional change, it is usually the result of one of the following human dynamics:

- People possessing inadequate skills for functioning in the new state;
- People being "left in the dark" and feeling uncertain about what is coming next;
- People's lack of understanding of the case for change or the benefits of the new state;
- People's reluctance to stop doing what they have always done in the past;
- Homeostasis or inertia—people's natural resistance to learning new skills or behaviors;

- People's emotional pain or grief at the loss of the past;
- Poor planning and implementation of the change, which creates confusion and resentment;
- Unclear expectations about what will be required to succeed in the new state;
- Fear about not being successful or capable in the new state; and/or
- Inadequate support to succeed in the new state.

Many executives view their organization's transitional changes as purely technical or structural, even when the changes do have human or cultural impacts. Neglecting these impacts, or inadequately planning or communicating the change process, produces greater human trauma than this type of change necessarily dictates.

Strategies for Managing Transitional Change

With the right transitional change strategies, the critical impacts of the change—organizational and human—can be dealt with effectively. Such strategies include a well-communicated case for change, a clear change plan, high employee involvement in designing and implementing that plan, local control of implementation, and adequate support and integration time to ensure that employees succeed in the new state.

A critical aspect of a transitional change strategy is to clarify the key differences between the old state and the desired state (similar to a gap analysis) and determine the implications of that gap. We call this process "impact analysis." An impact analysis assesses both organizational and human impacts and provides essential information for building a good change plan and reducing human trauma. The impact analysis reveals: (1) what aspects of the old state serve the new state and can be carried forward; (2) what aspects will need to be dismantled or dropped; and (3) what will need to be created from scratch to fit the needs of the new state. Conducting an impact analysis during the early stages of the transition state will indicate how much change is actually required and determine how long the transition will likely take. From this knowledge, leaders can develop a logical plan of action and appropriate timetable to guide the implementation of the new state.

Beckhard and Harris (1987) recommend managing the transition phase through two parallel and separate structures—one that keeps the operation running effectively and one that oversees the change, including the design of the new state, the impact analysis, and implementation planning. This is still an extremely effective approach for transitional change.

Transformational Change

Transformational change (shown in Figure 2.1 and outlined in Table 2.1) is the least understood and most complex type of change facing organizations today. Simply said, transformation is the radical shift from one state of being to another, so significant that it requires a shift of culture, behavior, and mindset to implement successfully and sustain over time. In other words, transformation demands a shift in human awareness that completely alters the way the organization and its people see the world, their customers, their work, and themselves. In addition, the new state that results from the transformation, from a content perspective, is largely uncertain at the beginning of the change process and emerges as a product of the change effort itself. Therefore, the transformation litmus test is found in these two basic questions:

1. Does your organization need to begin its change process before its destination is fully known and defined?

2. Is the scope of this change so significant that it requires the organization's culture and people's behavior and mindsets to shift fundamentally in order to implement the changes successfully and succeed in the new state?

If the answer is "yes" to either of these questions, then you are likely undergoing transformation. If the answer is "yes" to both, then you are definitely facing transformational change.

As we saw in the Drivers of Change Model, organization change stems from changes in the environment or marketplace, coupled with the organization's inability to perform adequately using its existing strategy, organizational design, culture, behavior, and mindset. The pain of the mismatch between the organization (including its human capability) and the needs of its environment creates a wake-up call for the organization. Ultimately, if the leaders of the organization do not hear or heed the wake-up call, and the organization does not change to meet the new demands, the organization will struggle. To thrive, the leaders must hear the wake-up call, understand its implications, and initiate a transformation process that attends to all the drivers of change.

In developmental change, simply improving current operations is adequate. In transitional change, replacing current operations with new, clearly defined practices suffices. But in transformational change, the environmental and marketplace changes are so significant that a profound breakthrough in people's worldview is required to even *discover* the new state with which they must replace current operations.

In developmental and transitional change, leaders can manage the change process with some semblance of order and control. They know where they are going and they can plan with greater certainty how to get there. In transformation, the change process has a life of its own and, at best, leaders can influence and facilitate it. If they attempt to control it, they will stifle creativity and progress. The "order" of the future state emerges out of the "chaos" of the transformational effort itself. Transformation, in fact, is the emergence of a new order out of existing chaos. Chaos, as used here, refers to the increasingly unstable dynamics of the organization as its current form disintegrates and is no longer as functional as it once was. The resulting new state is the product of both this chaos and the process that ensues to create a better future.

The Transformation Process

The story of the Phoenix rising from the ashes is a great metaphor for the transformation process. At the risk of oversimplification, the generic transformational process begins with ever-increasing disruption to the system, moves to the point of death of the old way of being, and then, as with the Phoenix, proceeds toward an inspired rebirth. Applied to the organization, the generic process goes something like this: An organization is initially born out of a new idea that serves the needs of its environment. In serving these needs, it grows and matures until it reaches a level of success. The organization works hard to maintain its success and, over time, functions on a plateau of sustained performance. Keeping the status quo is its primary goal in this phase. This is the period in which vibrant, entrepreneurial, and innovative organizations often turn bureaucratic and staid as they try to hold on to their current success. In the early 1980s, Apple Computer was a great example of this. Once successful, Apple's creative, entrepreneurial, fly-by-the-seat-of-your-pants culture gave way to bureaucratic controls required to run the organization more effectively. As necessary as this was, it squelched people's creativity.

Over time, most organizations on the success plateau begin to experience difficulties in any number of areas: hovering stock price, stagnation in product development, equipment failure and obsolescence, productivity drops, loss of control over costs and information, dips in employee morale, threats from competition, inadequate resources and skills, loss of market share, or relentless customer demands. These difficulties are all wake-up calls signaling the need for change. Often, leaders' attachment to the old ways that brought them success, coupled with their fear of the unknown, causes them to deny, explain away, or overlook these wake-up calls. Consequently, the calls get louder, more painful, and more costly.

As these difficulties increase, the organization moves into a period of struggle between internally and externally driven chaos. Finally, leaders wake up and attempt various "fix-it" initiatives to maintain some semblance of order and control. Some leaders respond by trying harder at what brought them initial success, but this only perpetuates the pain and further deepens the hole they are in. Other leaders approach the problems from a developmental perspective, throwing training at the organization or trying to squeeze more performance out of their existing operations. Or they apply a Band-Aid® such as cost-cutting efforts with no tie to any real strategic intent. With insufficient responses to the wake-up calls, the disturbance level increases and the organization's performance drops until finally something snaps. The organization is either forced out of business or it hears the essential wake-up call to shift its worldview.

The true transformational moment occurs when the organization's leaders finally listen to the wake-up calls, which catalyzes a breakthrough in their awareness and beliefs. This expansion of their conscious awareness and increase in their understanding of what is required to move forward denotes the initial and required shift in the leaders' mindsets. This shift sets the internal conditions in motion for the leaders to see new options for responding to their external circumstances. They begin to formulate new intentions about what is possible and necessary for the organization and its people to thrive.

This breakthrough of awareness catalyzes the emergence of the Phoenix. The transforming organization rises out of the ashes of its old beliefs, behavior, and form to take on a new direction that, in its new world, raises its performance capability to a much greater level of effectiveness. Armed with new insight, leaders begin to see the possibility of an entirely new direction that better serves their marketplace. All efforts to design the new state are driven by the shift in mindset.

The leaders, and subsequently the rest of the organization,[1] come to recognize that their world is not as it once was and that now they must be and do something radically different, no matter how successful they have been. The leaders' shift in mindset enables them to transform how they think, behave, and lead. Not only do

---

[1]We don't mean to imply that "the breakthrough to new awareness, beliefs, and intentions" must begin, or always begins, with the top leaders. Quite often, employees come to this realization long before the leaders do. Our point, however, is that *usually* enterprise-wise transformation does not get traction *until* the top leaders hear the wake-up call. Until that time, most leaders simply stifle employee-driven transformation. We must also note, however, that it is not uncommon to see the wake-up call for transformation emerging out of employee feedback to leaders about changing customer needs or from employee's changing work practices that generate substantial performance improvements as a result. Employees are often closer to the customer and the work and can play a vital role in initiating transformation.

they realize that they must create something entirely new in the organization, but they begin to see that they must approach the transformation in a completely new way. They also begin to acknowledge what is required of them personally to shepherd the process of moving forward. In short, they realize that their old ways won't work for their new challenge.

Examples of such profound shifts in mindset can be seen in the following: (1) When the executives of the leading American auto manufacturers finally realized that cars had to be smaller, better quality, and more fuel-efficient if they wanted to stay in business; (2) when the motivation and support for the war machine and nuclear arms buildup was becoming a lesser national priority and the defense industry had to adjust; and (3) when deregulation began to be a reality for the telephone, banking, gas, and electric utility industries and the certainty of selling their products and services for a guaranteed rate of return disappeared. In each of these cases, external events in the environment and marketplace catalyzed necessary shifts of mindset that brought on transformation. Not only did business practices change, but so did people's ways of working and relating to one another and customers— all because of the shift in mindset.

The leaders' shift in mindset also drives the cultural shifts that support the new business directions. Culture becomes an essential factor in the organization that is rising out of the ashes. The auto, defense, and utility industries could not have survived without radical culture change. In fact, all shared the requirement to break through their cultural mentality of "entitlement" and the assumption that whatever they produced would be sold or used. Today, for organizations in these "old economy" industries, the entrepreneurial, innovative, and self-determining mindset has become the foundation of their new culture and a driver of their current and future success.

For organizations born in the "new economy" of high-tech and the Internet, culture is equally critical. At first glance, however, we immediately notice that their cultures are vastly different. Speed, risk taking, innovation, and information sharing are cultural norms that old economy organizations are attempting to develop, whereas these norms already exist in many new economy businesses by the very fact that these businesses were created out of the fast-paced environment that requires these cultural norms. Although this may place some new economy businesses ahead of their old economy counterparts at this time, it does not mean that new economy businesses are without cultural challenges. Their challenges are just different. For instance, they may be challenged by the need to persuade employees who are focused on speed and innovation to slow down enough to mentor others. They may have difficulty persuading self-starters to adopt routine practices and standardization. They may have trouble establishing company loyalty and esprit de corps amid a workforce of "short timers" who are chasing the best employment contract. Creating high-performance cultural norms is a vital success factor in both old and new economy organizations.

Learning and Correcting Course

The journey of transformation is anything but a straight line. The process requires significant turns in the road because of the simple fact that it is full of uncertainty. This is for three reasons. First, because the future state is being discovered while the organization is going forward, the transformation process is literally the pursuit of an emerging target. As the target shifts, so must the process required to get there. Second, proceeding without a definitive destination requires heading into the unknown, which makes many people uncomfortable. When people react strongly to the unknown, their commitment and their performance level also become uncertain. Third, there is no way of knowing in advance the pace or actual scope of work required.

Figure 2.2 graphically portrays the journey of transformation. The vision of the transformation, which provides the general compass heading, determines the gap that must be closed between the organization's current state and its desired future. Notice how the classic change plan is drawn as a straight line, as if it can be rolled out without deviation. The change process (the actual journey) represents a vastly different path, making innumerable turns as the transformation unfolds.

How do you "manage" such an unpredictable and emergent process? First, give up any expectation of actually controlling the change process. Second, actively pursue information and feedback that signal a need to either alter your desired outcome or course of action. And third, optimize your ability to learn from the feedback you gather and turn that learning into efficient course corrections. Learning and course correcting are so essential for transformation that they could be its motto.

Most leaders tend to see deviation from the change plan as a tremendous problem. In transformation, deviation is never the problem. The issue is always about learning from the situation and then expediently changing course. The better the organization is at learning and course correcting—as individuals, teams, and a whole system—the smaller the adjustments need to be. Establishing learning and

Figure 2.2. Learning and Course Correction Model of Transformational Change

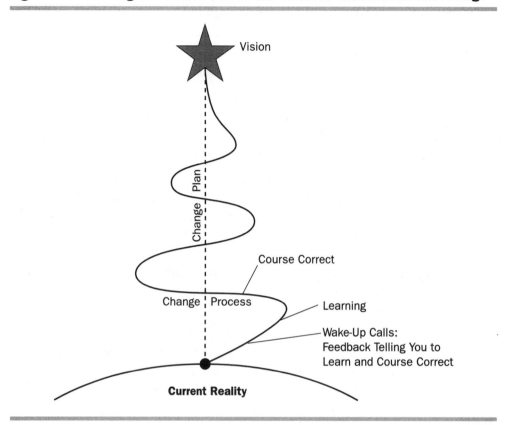

course correcting require building the skills and practices that support each. Furthermore, to develop comfort and expertise at learning and course correcting requires a significant change of mindset for most leaders and employees, which must be supported by appropriate shifts in cultural norms.

Human Dynamics in Transformation

Dealing with the chaos of transformation creates some interesting and challenging human dynamics. Because the process of figuring out and creating the new state is not highly controllable, organization members must be able to operate effectively within a heightened state of uncertainty and confusion. This presents the ultimate challenge: How to function effectively when you feel out of control and confused. Can people—executives, mid-managers, supervisors, and front-line employees alike—unite across differences to meet this challenge? Or will the uncertainty exacerbate their self-doubt, distrust, turf wars, and conflict?

Failure in transformation often results from the cancer of emotional immaturity and bad relationships made worse by the stress of marching into the unknown. When there is no definite answer about how to get where the organization needs to go, fear and blame can run rampant. Change leaders cannot stamp out or negate these predictable human reactions to the unknown, nor can they manage around them. However, they can—and must—create processes to support people to deal effectively with the unknown and, by doing so, assist these people to evolve as the organization determines its future. For this reason, organizational transformation strategies must include personal transformation strategies. Leaders must attend to people as much as they attend to content.

There are a number of high-leverage people strategies that must be incorporated into the overall change strategy. These can include personal growth training, dialogue, Appreciative Inquiry, coaching, team learning practices, profound benchmarking experiences, experiential education, frequent communications, and others.

Purpose, Vision, and Values During Transformation

Amid the uncertainty and change in transformation, the organization's "spirit"— its core purpose or unique reason for being—remains the same. The basic way the organization provides value to society endures. Its fundamental way of contributing to its customers and marketplace remains intact. In fact, during the height of the chaos of the organization's resurrection, the people of the organization must reflect on these critical questions: "What is our core purpose?" "What do we stand for? "What is our vision for serving the new marketplace needs?" To provide focus during the chaos, people need to remember why the organization is in business and what it stands for—its values. Organizations that lose touch with their core purpose, vision, and values have no inspiration to fuel their process of change. Without these, fear and panic can take over, causing leaders to "throw spaghetti at the wall" and try all sorts of new ventures, hoping that something will stick. By losing touch with themselves, they become rudderless ships in the night, diffusing their energies until they finally either sink or are taken over by an organization that has greater clarity.

Core purpose, along with shared vision and shared values, become the DNA that leaders can use to carry the organization from its past, through the uncertainty, into its tangible future. These factors guide the organization forward before tangible goals and outcomes can be identified. They align the organization and ensure that everyone remains emotionally connected and able to operate in the face of the challenges that could otherwise tear the organization apart. Rather than succumbing to the "comfort" of the old solutions, beliefs, and behaviors, clear purpose, vision, and values enable the organization to test new options without getting lost.

▶ CASE IN POINT

Detroit Edison experienced significant spiritual renewal when it reconnected to its core purpose, vision, and values early in its transformation. Not knowing the exact form that industry deregulation would take, or exactly when it would happen, and not knowing what new niche it should pursue to be successful in a competitive environment, the electric utility struggled mightily to re-create itself for the future. With no clear or inspiring direction, the organization was losing its footing and, in many ways, was adrift.

In response, the CEO and president together sponsored a two-day visioning offsite meeting for the top three hundred leaders in which the emotional uncertainty turned to excitement and hope. The group revisited the company's history and founding mission. They recalled their major successes and failures and relived their vibrant past. Together they challenged, debated, and ultimately re-ignited their ninety-year-old purpose in their own collective words. It now reads: "We energize the progress of society—we make dreams real—we are always here!"

In a staid electric utility culture, energizing the progress of society and making dreams real was quite inspirational. Remembering their vital role in their customers' lives boosted their confidence about their future. It expressed their rekindled vitality. As one leader put it, "Of course we will succeed and figure out a viable form for our contribution to society; by providing the energy to fuel dreams, we play a vital role in our community and the world." During chaos and uncertainty, such spiritual renewal is often exactly what is needed to mobilize unified action, out of which clarity of form can manifest. ◀

Personal Introspection in Transformation

Successful transformation requires a deeper dialogue among the people in the organization than is typical. It demands greater introspection into the very fabric of who the people of the organization are, what they stand for, and how they contribute to the larger environment they serve. Transformation calls for not only a new worldview, but a different way of being, working, and relating to meet the needs of the future state. If an organization neglects this deeper personal and cultural work in the early stages of its transformation, then chaos can consume the organization and the Phoenix will never rise. This is true for everyone in the organization, but especially for those leading and shaping the initial stages of the transformational process.

Clearly, transformation requires significant personal strength on the part of leaders to trust the wake-up calls for change and the personal and collective discovery process required for inventing a new way of being and operating in the organization. To do the personal work, leaders must possess significant internal fortitude. It takes internal discipline to lead the organization into the unknown and still remain confident. Leaders can experience profound angst when they hear the wake-up calls for radical change and then must confront their long-held beliefs about how to succeed. Quite often leaders feel an enormous burden during the prolonged uncertainty of the transformational change process.

It is not uncommon to hear executives who have stayed in the saddle during this turbulent period reflect on how much soul searching they did during the process. Feeling vulnerable, which is not frequently expressed in leadership circles, is common. Vulnerability goes hand-in-hand with leaders accepting that they do not have all of the answers and cannot control the process or outcome for which they feel so responsible. They must, in fact, have a significant degree of faith, trust, and commitment to proceed despite their concerns. When executives have climbed to the top of their success ladder through knowing what to do when and always being in control, facing the uncertainty of transformation is one of the toughest personal challenges of their professional lives. Often the toughest issue they face is the fact that perhaps their own beliefs, mindsets, or styles are the barriers to their organization's success. All of this internal reality has to be addressed openly.

Determining the Type of Change Taking Place

Every major change effort can be classified as one or the other of the three types of change. Often, one or both of the other types of change are present within the overall change, but are not as influential or paramount. For example, if a change is transformational, it is likely that both developmental and transitional changes will also be needed within the overall change process.

Exhibit 2.1 offers a questionnaire to help you determine which type of change the organization you are working with is facing. Remember that none of the types of change is more valuable than the others. Each serves a different need.

Exhibit 2.1. Determining the Type of Change Required

Instructions: Determine the primary type of change you are leading by answering the "litmus test" questions listed below. If you answer "yes" to two or more questions for one type of change, then that is the primary type of change you are facing. Remember to think of the overall change that is occurring, not the pieces within it. In most cases, all three types of change are occurring, but only one is primary.

Developmental Change Questions

1. Does your change effort *primarily* require an improvement of your existing way of operating, rather than a radical change to it?

2. Will skill or knowledge training, performance improvement strategies, and communications suffice to carry out this change?

3. Does your current culture and mindset support the needs of this change?

Transitional Change Questions

1. Does your change effort require you to dismantle your existing way of operating and replace it with something known but different?

2. At the beginning of your change effort, were you able to design a definitive picture of the new state?

3. Is it realistic to expect this change to occur over a pre-determined timetable?

Exhibit 2.1. Determining the Type of Change Required, Cont'd

Transformational Change Questions

1. Does your organization need to begin its change process before the destination is fully known and defined?

2. Is the scope of this change so significant that it requires the organization's culture and people's behavior and mindsets to shift fundamentally in order to implement the changes successfully and achieve the new state?

3. Does the change require the organization's structure, operations, products, services, or technology to change radically to meet the needs of customers and the marketplace?

Conclusions

1. Which of the three types of change is the primary type required?

2. Which of the other two types of change will also be needed to support this primary type? In what ways?

Summary

We have described three very different types of change operating in organizations, each of which requires different change strategies. Developmental and transitional changes are the most familiar and are easier to lead. Developmental change is the improvement of something that currently exists, while transitional change is the replacement of what is with something entirely new, yet clearly known. Both developmental and transitional change possess common characteristics: (1) Their outcomes can be quantified and known in advance of implementation; (2) significant culture, behavior, or mindset change is not required; and (3) the change process, its resource requirements, and the timetable, for the most part, can be managed.

The third type of change, transformation, requires a completely different set of change leadership skills. Transformation is the newest and most complex type of organization change, possessing very different dynamics: (1) The future state cannot be completely known in advance; (2) significant transformations of the organization's culture and of people's behavior and mindsets are required; and (3) the change process itself cannot be tightly managed or controlled because the future is unknown and the human dynamics are too unpredictable.

Transformation requires leaders to expand their worldview and increase their awareness and skill to include all the drivers of change, both external and internal. It requires a different mindset and style. And it demands that both leaders and employees undergo personal change as part of the organization's transformation. Over the years, we have seen two very different approaches to transformation from our clients. These approaches produce very different results. In the next chapter, we will describe these approaches and further clarify what transformation requires and what these requirements mean for leaders and consultants.

Two Leadership Approaches to Transformation

ⓘN THE LAST CHAPTER, WE IDENTIFIED three different types of change occurring in organizations. We explored the challenges they present, and clarified several strategies and outcomes for each. We also suggested that transformation requires full attention to both external "content" dynamics and the internal dynamics of people and culture. The Drivers of Change Model from Chapter One demonstrates the wide span of attention that transformation demands.

In this chapter, we identify what is required for leaders to expand their reach to include effective strategies for both the outer and the inner worlds of transformation. Specifically, we address how the state of awareness that leaders bring to transformation influences their approach to it. We define two very different approaches and explore each in depth. We also highlight many of the common mistakes that leaders and consultants make during transformation and reveal how their approach is the primary contributing factor to those mistakes as well as to their successes. Plus, we identify twenty-one critical dimensions to which leaders must attend to meet the demands of the internal and external aspects of successful transformation.

Two Approaches to Transformation

By *approach* to transformation, we mean the state of awareness that leaders personally bring to transformation and that influences the actions they take. The approach leaders take to transformation impacts every aspect of their change leadership capability and experience, including their personal ability to change, the change strategies they develop, their leadership and decision-making styles, their communication patterns, their relationships with stakeholders, their personal reactions, and ultimately, their outcomes. But mostly, leaders' approach determines what they are aware of and what they do not see.

In the simplest of terms, leaders either approach transformation with expanded awareness or limited awareness. We call the expanded awareness mode the "conscious" approach and the limited awareness mode the "reactive" (or unconscious) approach.

When leaders take the conscious approach, they have greater awareness about what transformation requires and the strategic options available to them to address its unique dynamics successfully. Expanded awareness is like getting the benefit of both a wide-angle lens and a high-powered telephoto lens at the same time. Through the wider view, leaders can see more broadly the dynamics at play in transformation. Through the telephoto view, they can see the deeper and more subtle dynamics that would otherwise go unnoticed. Expanded awareness provides both greater span and greater depth to their view.

When leaders take a reactive approach, they respond automatically and unconsciously to the dynamics of transformation based on their conditioned habits, existing knowledge, and dominant leadership style. Their lens is filtered, causing critical people and process dynamics to go unseen. They can only apply their old management techniques because their limited awareness offers them no other possibilities.

We do not want to imply that the reactive approach is "bad" or that leaders who use it are poor leaders. The reactive approach has sufficed for most leadership activities; it just isn't adequate for leading transformation. However, reactive leaders are doing the best they can with their limited awareness. They can't be blamed for not knowing what they don't know or not seeing what is outside the angle or power of their lens. The reactive approach to transformation and its patterns of behavior are described below in hopes of widening and strengthening the view of reactive leaders, making them more conscious and aware of the subtle dynamics of transformation and, therefore, making them better able to lead it.

The reactive approach to transformation has been most prevalent historically, while the conscious approach is becoming increasingly evident in today's organizations. As leaders acquire more experience with transformation, they are discovering more of what transformation entails and requires. Although there is much inertia to overcome, we believe that the conscious approach will dominate change leadership behavior in the 21st Century. In fact, from our perspective, the conscious approach is both the primary enabler of transforming today's organizations as well as successfully running tomorrow's.

In order to understand the two approaches thoroughly, let's first define "conscious" and "unconscious," then discuss the intra-personal dynamics of each. Later in the chapter, we will outline the different behaviors that reactive and conscious change leaders display.

Conscious vs. Unconscious

We define the term *conscious* as possessing conscious awareness; witnessing your experience; reflecting; being alert, clear-minded, observant. Being conscious is being *aware that you are aware.* Perhaps the most direct way of describing what we mean by "conscious" is to describe what it is not. In our application, we *could* easily use the word "unconscious" as the opposite of conscious. However, this would be misleading without an explanation of terms. Our use of unconscious would not mean "without awareness," as in someone who has been "knocked unconscious" or who is asleep. Instead, in our definition, unconscious would mean *without conscious awareness,* as with people who are awake and alert, yet not *consciously* aware of themselves, their behavior, their impact, the motivation for their choices, or what is going on around them.

A common example of this use of the term "unconscious" is a phenomenon that happens to many people as they drive down the freeway, especially if they drive the same route regularly. You have likely had the experience of driving down the highway and when the sign announcing your desired off-ramp catches your attention, you realize that you have been driving on autopilot, without any conscious awareness of your surroundings. You have been lost in your own thoughts. Your eyes have been open. You have been taking in information, yet processing it "unconsciously." Then, when you pop back into conscious awareness, you are startled by the fact that you have been driving for so long without any memory of the scenery or the cars around you. You are surprised because you did not "witness" any of your experience.

For us, being "conscious" equates to moments when you are witnessing what fills your awareness, while "unconscious" (reactive) refers to those moments when you are on autopilot.

The Witness and the Autopilot

Conscious awareness (the witness) and unconscious awareness (the autopilot) are literally two different states of consciousness. In both, we are aware, taking in information from our environment. In the witness state, we are *consciously* aware of information as our senses collect it. On autopilot, however, the information enters our system and we respond automatically and unconsciously, without witnessing the information or our response.

This subtle, yet profound aspect of intra-personal reality is quintessentially important to change leaders. Why? Because transformation requires that leaders more deeply understand people and process dynamics; increasing their ability to witness their experience promotes that understanding. When leaders are consciously aware, they can inquire into and penetrate more deeply the subtle dynamics at play. They can question, investigate, and learn about them. On autopilot, however, leaders do not have this opportunity. They simply see what they see at face value and react accordingly.

Furthermore, activating their "inner witness" increases leaders' ability to notice and stop their automatic habitual reactions to situations that call for new transformational behaviors and strategies. When they are witnessing their experience, they can consciously choose their response. In autopilot, however, leaders' response is predetermined by their conditioning. Plus, with conscious awareness, leaders can think "outside the box" and consciously design strategies for responding to their situations. Unconscious awareness, however, can only deliver leaders' current skills and capabilities because their response happens automatically without conscious intervention.

For most leaders, the distinction between the witness and autopilot goes unnoticed. With their focus so dominantly on external reality, they do little to explore their internal reality.

The best way to understand this phenomenon is to directly experience it. Try an experiment with us. Focus on something in your current environment—a visual object, the weight of your body against your chair, or your breath going in and out. Focus on this object for four or five minutes (longer if you choose) and bring your awareness back whenever it wanders.

What did you experience? Most likely, when you began, you were consciously aware of the object. Then after a while, your mind wandered and you lost conscious awareness of the object. In fact, you likely lost conscious awareness of everything. Instead, you were lost in thought or focused elsewhere without realizing it until you "woke up." Then, again consciously aware, you brought your awareness back to the object until you slipped back into autopilot, once again lost in thought or unconsciously focused on other objects. Each time you went off, you would, at some point, become consciously aware that you were off and then return to the desired object of focus.

This oscillation in and out of conscious awareness goes on continuously, every day, every hour, every minute. The key to the conscious approach is expanding the amount of time that you are consciously aware and the frequency of "waking up" so you can use that awareness to develop your capacity to lead transformation successfully.

Like all capabilities, you can develop and strengthen this ability over time. As you exercise your witness and bring yourself to conscious awareness throughout your day, this state will grow stronger within you. Various meditation techniques and self-mastery processes are the most direct methods. A disciplined daily practice is optimal. In the next chapter, we will discuss some of these practices briefly. However, the practice of self-mastery techniques is not the topic of this particular book, so we will not go into great detail. Our intention is to bring the importance of conscious awareness to light for leaders of transformation.

Building Change Leadership Competency

The Competency Model (see Figure 3.1) highlights the role of conscious awareness in learning and performance. We will apply this model to leading transformation by telling the story of how a leader moves through each of the four stages of development.

Reactive leaders begin at the first stage. They are initially "unconsciously incompetent"—they don't know what they don't know. Not understanding transformation and its unique requirements, they assume their current knowledge, skills, and leadership or consulting practices (for developmental or transitional change) will suffice. Then, as they begin to hear the wake-up calls demonstrating that their strategies for leading transformation are not working well, they become "consciously incompetent." They now realize that they do not possess the knowledge and skill they need.

Figure 3.1. Competency Model*

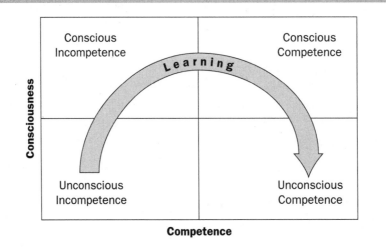

*Variations of this model have been widely used in organization development and human resource circles for years. Our exhaustive Internet search did not identify the originator(s).

This personal insight can begin the reactive leader's process of becoming more conscious. Leaders who have a high psychological need to be perceived as right and competent typically become very uncomfortable at this point. Rather than pursue the necessary learning, they may deny their need and instead put on the façade of competence. These leaders remain reactive, never increasing their conscious awareness or understanding of what transformation really requires. They remain "unconsciously incompetent," held back by their own personal denial and their delusion of being sufficiently capable. They stay stuck in autopilot.

Other leaders, however, hear the wake-up call to increase their awareness and understanding of transformation and take this need seriously. They commit to learning, some about the external dynamics of transformation, others about the internal dynamics as well.

The internally oriented learners realize that learning about transforming their organizations requires them to explore their own leadership biases, beliefs, and assumptions. They begin to be introspective, to reflect on their own behaviors, and to inquire into their beliefs about organizations, people, and change. In doing so, they encounter the witness/autopilot phenomenon and begin to notice their "automatic and unconscious" reactions. As they begin to catch themselves operating on autopilot more frequently, they are able to increase the time they operate consciously.

Over time, both types of learners become "consciously competent" in their chosen areas of focus; they become able to perform their learned change leadership behaviors and strategies as long as they are consciously thinking about them and witnessing what they are doing. However, the leaders who have turned inward and are pursuing greater conscious awareness learn faster and learn about deeper, more subtle aspects of transformation. Their learning is more complete.

At this stage, both types of learners may frequently fall back into operating unconsciously, on autopilot, applying their old behaviors and management practices to transformation. However, the leaders who have made the commitment to pursue greater conscious awareness have a new capability. When someone makes them consciously aware that they are operating reactively, on autopilot, they accept this feedback. In fact, they want this feedback, even seek it. They want to be awakened because they realize that operating more consciously will deliver greater results. This new behavior further increases their learning.

As both types of learners persevere in their practice, they reach the desirable stage of becoming "unconsciously competent," able to perform the behaviors and tasks they have learned without deliberate thought. The difference between the two is simply what they have learned. The externally oriented learners have a greater repertoire of actions and strategies, while the internally oriented learners also possess deeper insight about how to use them effectively.

Furthermore, for the internally oriented learners, the learning never stops. The fruits of taking a conscious approach have become obvious, and they continue to strengthen their capacity to witness their experience consciously. This continually produces new insights for them about both external and internal dynamics, furthering their change leadership skill.

Wake-Up Calls for Transformation

In order to acquire the insight and skill in both the internal (people) and external (content) aspects of transformation, leaders must first hear and assimilate four levels of wake-up calls, described in Figure 3.2. The levels show increasing magnitudes of awareness and the typical sequence in which change leadership awareness develops. The figure shows these levels as a hierarchy of nested frames, the first included within the second, which is included within the third, and so on.

Figure 3.2. Levels of Wake-Up Calls for Transformation

The first level of wake-up call is the easiest for leaders to hear. It is the recognition that the status quo in the organization no longer works and that a change is required. The second level of wake-up call is the realization that the change is transformational. This level requires that leaders understand that the process of transformation is uniquely different from that of developmental or transitional change.

The third level of wake-up call, certainly more of a stretch, is the realization that transformation requires new strategies and practices. This wake-up call triggers the leadership breakthrough that is necessary for successful transformation. It usually starts with the insight that traditional leadership approaches and change management practices are not sufficient for transformational change.

The fourth level of wake-up call, the most far-reaching and eye-opening, is the realization that transformation requires leaders to change *personally*, that they must change their mindsets, behaviors, and styles to lead transformation successfully. This is the level of wake-up call that turns the focus of leaders' attention into themselves. Externally oriented leaders do not get this wake-up call; internally oriented leaders do. This wake-up call carries the insight that within leaders' own consciousness lie the source of both their current limitations and failures as well as future breakthroughs and successes. Leaders realize that without putting themselves overtly into their organization's change process, the full potential of the transformation will not manifest. They now acknowledge that they must transform themselves to become a model of the desired change. Upon hearing the level-four wake-up call, leaders have entered the world of conscious transformation and the increased results it can generate.

▶ CASE in POINT

John Lobbia, the ex-CEO of Detroit Edison, quickly moved through three levels to the fourth, perhaps faster than any CEO we had worked with previously. When we met John, he was very clear that his organization had to change (Level One) to meet the challenges of deregulation in the electric utility industry. A brilliant man, John's gut instinct was that the change required was transformational (Level Two); he knew that his organization needed to begin its change long before he or anyone else could be certain about its future state and that the change needed was so significant that the organization's culture and the behavior and mindsets of its leaders and employees would need to transform to sustain the mammoth content changes required. Initially, John did not realize that his and his leaders' old approaches, strategies, and mindsets would not suffice for this transformation. However, with a bit of coaching, he quickly saw the obvious (Level Three). To share his insights with his top leaders, he agreed to sponsor a training session called the "Transformational Leadership Program."

Perhaps the most endearing moment of working with John and his executive team came during this training session when it truly hit John that his organization's transformation required *him* to change *personally* (Level Four). As John stated to his team so pointedly, "I have been so focused on us *surviving* deregulation that I haven't attended to how we could *thrive* in a deregulated environment. I've been operating in a mindset that there won't be enough success to go around in the future and, therefore, we need to protect what we now have. But I see that this defensive orientation is only in my mindset. The fact is that we have more than enough talent, resources, and commitment to create a very successful future. Let's pursue growth, not stability."

John's "breakthrough" of insight that his own mindset was limiting his organization catalyzed tremendous growth for his company. In John's words: "Soon after that session, we adopted a growth goal of building new businesses that would generate $100 million in net income in five years. This is the fifth year [2000] and the new businesses will earn over $100 million this year. Quite a success."

John's insight that his mindset was limiting his perspective for the organization triggered significant personal introspection. By "witnessing" the impact of his internal reality on his decisions and actions as CEO, John became very committed to bringing the inner human dimension of transformation into Detroit Edison's change effort. Mammoth transformation ensued at Detroit Edison, with John initiating the way through his own dedicated efforts to become more consciously aware, change his style, and model the transformation he was asking of his organization. ◄

In our discussions of both the Competency Model and the Levels of Wake-Up Calls for Transformation (Figures 3.1 and 3.2), we have emphasized the critical role of expanding conscious awareness. In short, *we believe that change leaders' ability to lead transformation successfully is dependent on becoming more aware of both the external and internal dynamics of transformation and the options and strategies available for influencing them. Furthermore, this requires engaging and strengthening one's "inner witness" and ability to maintain conscious awareness.*

Now let's explore how both the reactive and conscious approaches to leading transformation impact change leadership behavior.

The Reactive Approach

As we said earlier, the reactive approach to leading transformation is by far the most common. Leaders who respond reactively do not do so intentionally, but rather *unknowingly*. In fact, they simply don't think about it. External events happen, and they react to them in habitual ways, automatically, without conscious intention.

Reactive leaders typically do not differentiate the types of change they face and therefore do not understand transformational change as different. They react to the need to change without conscious thought or reflection, and because they do not see the more subtle people and process dynamics of transformation, they overlook critical change leadership strategies. Inevitably, these unintentional oversights restrict their success and are usually the source of their failures.

Reactive leaders are limited to approaching transformation based on their current conditioning, beliefs, leadership style, and tried-and-true leadership practices, without knowing that those practices are inadequate to the task. These leaders are trapped within their current understanding and conditioning. One major habitual response is how they deal with—or don't deal with—the signals for the need to change.

Reactive leaders are not very open to hearing wake-up calls, especially levels three and four. Most people tend to avoid what makes them uncomfortable, and change makes reactive leaders very uncomfortable, especially personal change. Therefore, because they are not conscious of their reactions, reactive leaders automatically resist or explain away the signals for change, without even being aware that they are doing so.

Reactive leaders typically have a strong denial mechanism. For organizations led by reactive leaders, it is usually the marketplace's heightened threat to their survival that becomes the level-one wake-up call that the leaders finally hear. The signal, by this time, is usually cataclysmic and harsh. Because the signals have been ignored for so long, the situation is graver than it would have been with an earlier response. The organization is finally forced to face its transformational reality. Instantly, reactive leaders feel out of control, resentful, and burdened by the formidable challenge of change they now face. They feel pressured to proceed and immediately want to get through the disruption as quickly as possible. They will change because they have to, not because they want to. Their primary motivation is to take away the pain and regain their comfort and sense of control.

When reactive leaders hear the level-one wake-up call and acknowledge the need to change, they often respond with developmental or transitional change strategies because they are familiar with them and do not yet appreciate the differences among the three types of change or the strategies they each require. They will typically attempt classic problem-solving and project-management techniques, training, and improving communications, each of which has value, but is not sufficient for leading transformation.

Reactive leaders attend mostly to the surface symptoms they face, seldom addressing the underlying root causes. Their superficial efforts may create temporary relief but, ironically, can also increase the pressure and likelihood for a transformational breakdown because they address neither the systemic causes of the upheaval nor provide real change solutions.

In their attempts to gain control, reactive leaders often initiate any one of numerous "flavor of the month" change programs, hoping that something good will stick. Perhaps the worst case of this reactive approach is found in the senior executive who returns from the latest management seminar or reads the most recent best-selling management book (even this one) and declares to the organization, "We are going to re-engineer!" (or do quality, or install self-directed teams, or implement new information technology, or change the culture). In the best of these cases, the leaders search for safe, proven solutions or best practices that have worked for other organizations. For example, many reactive leaders design their new organization as a reflection of some other organization's solution, hoping that it will work for them, too, but it seldom does. Such blatant reactive responses, not thought out nor customized to the unique needs of the organization, damage leadership credibility in the eyes of employees and catalyze tremendous resistance.

Because of their urgent need for certainty, reactive leaders are prime targets for expert-oriented (content) consulting firms who seek out situations where their solutions with previous clients can be installed as "the answer." With varying degrees of success, they may attempt to implement transformational strategies such as business process reengineering, information technology solutions, fast cycle time, autonomous work groups, and flat organizational structures.

Are these strategies guaranteed answers just because they worked elsewhere under different circumstances? Certainly not, although aspects of such strategies can be of tremendous value. Reactive leaders fall prey to attempting these strategies without *consciously* thinking about the fit with their organization's unique circumstances. They often tell the expert consultants, "Just go do it." However, a good solution applied to the wrong problem is still a mistake. A bit of healthy introspection would go a long way to limit the negative effects of such unconscious reactions.

In the 1980s and early 1990s, the rash of business diversification efforts in corporate America was a clear sign of the reactive approach to change. Profitable organizations whose futures were threatened bought organizations they had no business buying, just to hedge against an unknown future. This scatter-shot approach to creating a future that could survive the tumultuous changes in the business environment was a hope-filled but panicked reaction. Oil companies ventured into the transportation business, donuts, and copy machines. Insurance companies expanded into real estate, training, and consulting. It's not that these ventures might not prove to be lucrative; they just were not what the purchasing organizations knew or excelled in. These ventures nearly always proved to be great distractions from the critical question facing the leaders: How can we maintain our purpose and transform our core business to compete successfully in our new marketplace?

When organizations adopt the business strategy of becoming a holding company, diversification of this nature might work. However, when they retain their original identity, this diversification strategy usually dilutes their resources and focus, reducing their success.

Another major issue with the reactive approach is that leaders may recognize the change required in the business' strategy or organizational design, but not in the culture or leadership style—and certainly not in their own behavior or thinking. Although reactive leaders may believe that personal or behavioral change is needed for the rest of the organization, they often refuse to acknowledge that they have to change themselves. They are already exceedingly uncomfortable because their need for control has been threatened, so exploring their own mindsets, styles, and behavior furthers that discomfort by making them more vulnerable. *Reactive leaders' unwillingness to see that they need to transform themselves in order to transform their organizations is often the biggest stumbling block to their organization's successful transformation.*

Impact on Employee Morale

The morale of the employees who work for organizations run by reactive leaders is often very low. We have witnessed numerous situations in which the employees see the need for transformation and want the company to transform, but their leaders either deny the need to change or can't see the true scope of what needs to change or how to make the change happen. Employees on the front lines directly experience the disruption caused by their leaders' denial or inadequate change plans. Employees can often recognize—long before their leaders—that the leaders' strategies for transformation have little chance for success. Employees feel threatened because they believe that their future rests on the organization's ability to transform successfully and they don't see success as a likely outcome.

Another reason for low employee morale in reactive efforts is that their leaders often toss numerous uncoordinated and non-integrated change efforts at the organization with no context given for why they are needed nor a way to integrate them into something that has impact. Employees feel like they are spinning their wheels. They see gaps and overlaps between these change initiatives and resent the poor planning and duplication of effort they require.

Perhaps the biggest reason for low morale is that reactive leaders add change-related work to employees' already full plates. Daryl R. Conner (1998) describes this phenomenon well: "When change continues to be poured into a saturated sponge, the consequences are threefold: (a) morale deteriorates; (b) the initiatives that are attempted result in only short-term, superficial application of the intended goals; and (c) people stop listening to the leaders, who continue to announce changes that never fully materialize" (p. 15).

Most Common Mistakes

The result of all this is that reactive leaders cause and repeat many of the common mistakes we see in leading transformation. Their most common mistakes include:

- Exerting too much top-down control over the design of the future state and the change process;
- Viewing the transformation as an event or an isolated problem to be fixed, rather than as a complex and evolving process;
- Neglecting culture, behavior, and mindset, both in employees and in themselves;
- Misdiagnosing the scope of change required, such as focusing only on organizational design or technology upgrades;
- Mandating the change, which squelches participation and increases employee resistance;
- Taking a short-term, minimalist approach to change, as in trying to do the least possible in the shortest amount of time;
- Setting unrealistic, crisis-producing timelines; and/or
- Poor modeling and not walking the talk; asking the workforce to change in certain ways and then continuing old behavior themselves.

The most direct way for leaders to avoid these common mistakes in leading transformation is to become more self-reflective and conscious, hear all four levels of wake-up calls, and learn how to deal more effectively with what transformational change requires. Let's now explore the conscious approach to see how it better prepares leaders to lead transformation.

The Conscious Approach

For all the reasons we have discussed, conscious leaders are more aware of the subtleties and unique dynamics of transformation, including both human and process, and they use their awareness to develop advanced competencies and create innovative change strategies.

Conscious leaders have the potential to match their walk to their talk, even when their talk forces them outside their comfort zones. Because they are cognizant of the strengths and weaknesses of their own mental models and behaviors, conscious leaders are able to acknowledge the shortcomings in their current approaches more readily, thus allowing them to choose more effective alternatives.

Being conscious does not, however, automatically improve leaders' mental models, alter their behavior, or undo their bad habits—nor does it stop all the unwanted surprises that are a part of most transformation efforts. However, when surprises do occur, conscious leaders are able to respond effectively to them because the strength of their "inner witness" keeps them from becoming swallowed up by their reactions to the challenge.

Conscious leaders' expanded awareness helps them minimize their risk of being blindsided by change-related problems that could negatively impact their results. Because they hear wake-up calls earlier, conscious leaders maximize their ability to correct their transformational change strategies as they go. They are more alert to both what is and is not working well and can amplify the positive and improve on the negative more expediently.

Although reactive leaders operate in reaction to their environment, conscious leaders understand that they work in partnership with their environment. Wake-up calls from the environment are welcome feedback for them and help to guide their decisions and actions. In fact, conscious leaders intentionally expand their awareness by actively seeking wake-up calls for change, as we will see later in this chapter.

Twenty-One Dimensions of Conscious Transformation

We stated in the introduction to this book that we believe in a "multi-dimensional" approach to leading transformation and suggested that conscious leaders must attend to both external and internal reality and possess both content and people expertise. Here we further develop these ideas. This concept can be expanded to twenty-one critical dimensions that change leaders must become conscious of and competent to address (see Figure 3.3). Some of these critical dimensions are external, some internal.

Figure 3.3. Twenty-One Dimensions of Conscious Transformation

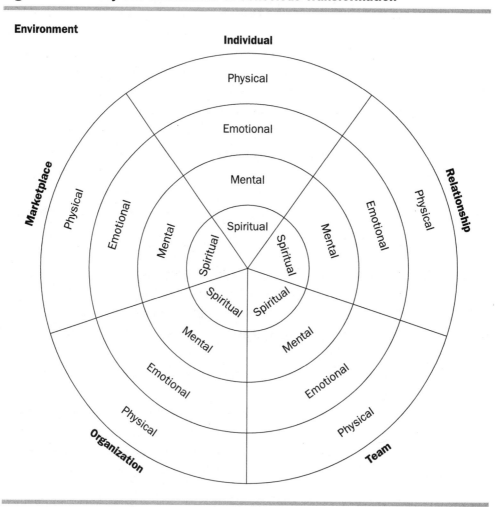

The Levels

The five pie slices in Figure 3.3 represent different levels of how people "organize." The smallest unit of organization is, of course, the *individual*. Individuals come together with other individuals and establish *relationships*. When a small collective of individuals come together, a group or *team* is formed. Multiple teams collectively create an *organization*. Multiple organizations form an industry or *marketplace*. The five levels form a hierarchy. As Ken Wilber (1998, p. 67) describes hierarchies, "Each successive unit *transcends* but *includes* its predecessors. Each senior element contains or enfolds its juniors as components in its own makeup, but then adds something *emergent*, distinctive, and defining that is not found in the lower level: it transcends and includes." Wilber continues, "Each element is a *whole* that is simultaneously a *part* of another whole."

In other words, individuals, who are wholes themselves, are simultaneously the parts of relationships. Relationships, which are also wholes, are parts of teams, and so forth. Each element is neither just a part nor just a whole, but *both, a part/whole*. This characteristic is an important insight that conscious change leaders must understand.

The Domains

Within each of these levels of organization, there exist four domains of human experience, represented by the *physical, emotional, mental,* and *spiritual. Physical* reality is the domain in which tangible forms or structures exist. *Emotional* reality is the world of qualitative feelings. *Mental* reality consists of thoughts, judgments, assumptions, and beliefs. *Spiritual* reality is the domain of meaning, purpose, and connectedness to the whole of life. The physical domain is, of course, external reality, while internal reality is comprised of the mental, emotional, and spiritual domains.

Most people would agree that these four domains exist within individuals. However, they also exist within every level of organization! For example, teams have physical forms, determined by their membership, governance structure, roles, responsibilities, and work processes. Teams certainly have feeling states; sometimes there is conflict and strife within the team, while at other times there is cooperation and harmony. Teams also possess collective expectations, mental agreements, and thought processes for how to perform their work. And finally, teams possess a purpose—a reason for being and a unique way they contribute value to the larger organization—which expresses the team's spirit.

These same four domains of reality exist at the organizational level. Organizations have structures, systems, technology, processes, and policies (physical forms); they have morale and esprit de corps (emotions); they possess strategies, mental models, collective norms, and agreements about good or bad behavior (thoughts); and they have purpose in serving the larger marketplace in inherently valuable ways (spiritual meaning).

So, we have five levels of organization, each possessing four domains of human experience, which makes twenty dimensions. The twenty-first dimension is represented by the environment.

How the Twenty-One Dimensions Operate

Change leaders must realize that these twenty-one dimensions exist, that they have an impact on their organization's transformations, and that they must all be attended to. Leaders must also understand four critical dynamics about how these dimensions interact in order to influence any of them optimally during change.

1. Influence Moves Up and Down the Levels. Every part is an aspect of, and influenced by, the wholes above it, just as every whole is comprised of, and influenced by, the parts below it. All levels have impact in both directions, and none can be ignored.

For example, change leaders cannot just attend to organizational dynamics (the whole) in order to improve organizational performance. They must also attend to the dynamics that are occurring within the teams, relationships, and individuals who exist within their organization (the parts). Poor performance at any level will roll up into poor performance in the higher levels. Similarly, change leaders must look to the marketplace dynamics and at what is happening nationally and internationally for things that might influence their organization's success (the greater wholes).

2. Where a Dimension Exists in the Hierarchy Establishes Its Relevance and Meaning. Every part/whole has both relevance and meaning. Relevance is how a part/whole contributes to the viability of higher levels—how it fits into the larger picture and serves the larger systems. If a part/whole loses its relevance, it becomes extinct, so to speak, because it no longer serves a larger purpose. For example, if an organization loses touch with changes in its marketplace, it may lose its relevance and not produce enough of what its customers want to remain a viable business. If a work team does not produce what is needed by the organization, then it loses its relevance and will be disbanded. Each part/whole must look up to maintain pace with changes occurring in the higher levels to ensure its relevance and viability.

Meaning is derived from the intrinsic value a part/whole places on its relevance. For example, a work team has relevance in how it serves the organization, but if the team is not inspired by this purpose, it will not be motivated to perform. Team members find *relevance* by looking up and *meaning* by looking inside themselves.

To maintain a high performing system at any level of organization, each part/ whole must have both relevance and meaning.

3. Influence Moves in All Directions Across the Domains of a Level. Any positive or negative shift in any domain will ripple across the other domains, regardless of the level. For example, achieving a company-wide goal (physical form) can enliven an organization's morale (emotional state), reinforce the collective norms that delivered the high performance (mental agreements), and create a sense of meaning and spiritual renewal for the company. Similarly, a crisis of meaning can send an individual into emotional upheaval, generate negative self-talk, and cause him or her to perform poorly.

4. All Twenty-One Dimensions Are Interconnected and Form One Multi-Dimensional System. Shifts in any one dimension can create related shifts in any or all of the others. For example, shifts in the marketplace requirements for success can cause an organization to redesign its structure or re-engineer its business processes, which in turn can impact employee morale, alter cultural norms, cause teams to change their membership, trigger anxiety in individuals, shift the collective agreements about how work gets done, break up longstanding working relationships, cause individual employees to lose their jobs, and so on.

This interdependent, whole systems reality represents an expanded way of viewing organizations for most leaders. We will explore this worldview in great detail in Chapter Five. For now, suffice it to say that leaders and consultants of transformation must expand their conscious awareness and intuitive understanding of each of these twenty-one dimensions and become conscious of the dynamic relationships that exist between and among them. This, essentially, is the heart of the conscious approach to transformation.

Exhibit 3.1 is a worksheet that can be used to help you to assess how the twenty-one dimensions affect your organization.

Marketplace Dynamics

Although conscious leaders must attend to all twenty-one dimensions, three general areas are most critical: *marketplace* dynamics, *people* dynamics, and *process* dynamics. These three areas are the key leverage points for conscious leaders, providing the greatest sources of potential breakthrough in understanding and skill that can catapult their change leadership—and their organizations—to new levels

Exhibit 3.1. Worksheet to Assess How the Twenty-One Dimensions Affect Your Organization

This worksheet can help you identify which of the twenty-one dimensions of conscious transformation are impacting your change effort at the present time. The matrix below lists all of the dimensions, including all four of the domains of the environment. Therefore, there are twenty-four boxes in the matrix, instead of twenty-one.

Consider the transformation you are consulting to or leading. Identify an actual situation or set of circumstances that you are currently facing or an issue you must address. Focus on this aspect of the transformation and consider the dynamics at play within it at all levels of organization and for all domains of experience. Fill in the dynamics you have actually observed that have an impact on the situation or that you know will impact its resolution. Jot down a few words or phrases in the boxes to capture what you observe. Leave the boxes blank that do not pertain.

Levels	Domains			
	Physical	**Emotional**	**Mental**	**Spiritual**
Individual/Self				
Relationship				
Team				
Organization				
Marketplace				
Environment				

Which dimensions are critically interdependent?

Which three dimensions require the most attention at this time?

What interventions would positively impact those dimensions?

of success. Section Two of the book focuses on the essence of *people* dynamics— mindset. Section Three thoroughly attends to *process* dynamics. We'll briefly overview the conscious approach to *marketplace* dynamics here.

Although reactive leaders *react* to their marketplace and environment, conscious leaders seek to *foretell* and help create the future of their marketplace and environment. While reactive leaders get pushed around by their marketplaces' wake-up calls for change, conscious leaders attempt to discover the subtle meanings that lie within these wake-up calls. They want to know what is *causing* them, not simply see their effect.

Conscious leaders inquire into the root cause of wake-up calls from their marketplace or environment because they know that they may be a signal of an emerging paradigm or trend in their industry. They want to be the first to discover what new order is trying to emerge so they can be the first to respond to it.

After conscious leaders are clear about the emerging paradigm, they use its attributes as design requirements, establishing a template against which they can craft and assess possible future scenarios, such as creating a new business strategy or designing new products. These business strategies, of course, then feed into and drive their transformation strategies.

Conscious leaders realize that if they can figure out what the marketplace is moving toward, they can be the first to provide the new products or services it demands. Essentially, conscious leaders seek to usher the emerging paradigm into existence in both their marketplace and their organizations, thereby reaping the benefits of more directly and expediently meeting their customers' evolving needs.

Historically, Intel has been a great example of this market orientation. They use their product evolution strategy to create the next marketplace demand for what they alone can provide. Being ahead of the market has enabled Intel to use planned product obsolescence as a market expansion strategy. Not only have they read the market, but they have *made* the market in many cases!

Another profound example of marketplace dynamics was the shift in paradigm that occurred over the past few decades about the importance of customers. In the 1950s and 1960s, leaders seldom spoke of customers. Instead, market share was king. If an organization had market share, then customers could be (and were) taken for granted. All the organization had to do was produce quality widgets at a fair price and customers would automatically buy them—or so it was thought.

Over the past two decades, because competition, technology, and ever-changing marketplace dynamics are always reshuffling the customer and marketplace deck, organizations have been undergoing transformation to become more customer-focused, service-oriented, and relationship-savvy. The need to be customer-centered has radically changed many organizations' business strategies, organizational structure, product configurations and design methodologies, marketing approaches, manufacturing processes, and culture. Conscious leaders who heard the wake-up call early and were the first to build customer-oriented organizations reaped huge benefits.

What happens to organizations in which leaders miss the paradigm shifts in their industries is evident. Recall the graphic stories from decades past of the Swiss watch manufacturers, the U.S. automobile manufacturers, and IBM, all of which neglected their industry's wake-up calls. In contrast, think of current visionary companies that are actively seeking to understand the future paradigm of their marketplace so they can lead their organizations into it. For example, consider:

- The e-commerce companies that are marketing their products via the Internet because they know that customers' lives are becoming increasingly hectic and that shopping ease and instant gratification are value-added services;

- The downtown gourmet, home delivery, "restaurants" that have created an industry out of making a quality dining experience easy;

- The handful of ninety-year-old utility companies that have ventured heavily into researching solar power, fuel cells, and bio-mass fuel generation because they understand that the paradigm of the future will demand sustainable resources and environmental protection;

- The Big Four consulting firms who are creating worldwide change management practices because they recognize that global companies will increasingly demand this service and that they are uniquely positioned to provide it;

- The health care providers and insurance companies that have realized the growing demand by health conscious baby boomers who are products of the 1960s for complementary care in the services they provide and for the integration of holistic wellness practices with allopathic medicine and disease prevention; and

- The companies that are using recycled goods to manufacture new products.

Companies with such insights about emerging paradigms that impact their industries may not become immediately profitable, but they enter the race as front-runners because of their conscious attention to understanding the deeper, more subtle dynamics of their marketplace and the world in which they live. True visionaries see an emerging paradigm long before the masses even notice, and conscious leaders have the greatest potential for visionary insight and action. By waking up and strengthening their inner witness, they can more easily catch themselves before they shrug off "out of the box" ideas or interpretations of new marketplace dynamics. Conscious leaders also typically have the moral and ethical motivation to do what is right for the good of the whole (organization, community, nation, planet) and will make changes for these long-term reasons, not just for immediate profit.

Do You Operate Consciously or Reactively?

Every human being has both a reactive side and a conscious side. There are times when people are reactive—unconscious—in their behavior and response to a situation, just as there are times when they are consciously aware and fully cognizant of their states of mind, what they are doing, their impact on others, and the options before them.

The reactive and conscious approaches to leading transformation form two ends of a continuum. Although all people have the capacity for both ways of being within them, at any point in time people's primary approach exists at some point along that continuum. As people grow, they move across the continuum, becoming less reactive and more conscious.

It may be difficult to determine where you are on this continuum, as the measurement is rather nebulous. One measurement to consider is the number of times during the day that you pause and consciously witness your experience in present time. Does this happen at all? Less than three times a day? Ten times? Fifty? Attending to the daily frequency in which you are consciously aware will strengthen your witness.

Moving yourself along the continuum is an essential change leadership development activity, one that requires dedication, commitment, and hard work. It is a continual process of self-discovery and learning, if you choose to engage in it. Essentially, becoming more conscious is a way of living life, not an end state.

Summary

In this chapter, we introduced the conscious approach to leading transformation and contrasted it with the more common reactive approach. We addressed the differences in the behavior of reactive and conscious change leaders, showing how the conscious approach is key to successful transformation. We addressed the critical source of the conscious approach—the intra-personal dynamic of conscious awareness—that increases change leaders' ability to "witness" what is occurring in transformation. We discussed the four levels of wake-up calls for transformation, revealing that change leaders must hear the Level-Four call and engage in transforming themselves to transform their organizations. We introduced the twenty-one dimensions of conscious transformation and how they operate as an interconnected, multi-dimensional system. We completed the chapter by discussing how conscious leaders continually scan their marketplace and environment to find evidence of a new paradigm emerging in their industry so they can be the first to respond to it.

This chapter has set the stage for the next section, where we will explore mind-set, first by discovering its role and impact in transformation and then by exploring the fundamental mental assumptions about reality that enable change leaders to see and respond to the dynamics of transformation more accurately.

Section Two
Mindset: The Leverage Point for Transformation

The Role and Impact of Mindset

ON SECTION ONE, WE PRESENTED AN OVERVIEW of the drivers of change to demonstrate that the majority of today's change is transformational, requiring leaders to attend to both internal and external dynamics. We also described the conscious approach to transformation, which fully acknowledges mindset as the primary enabler of successful transformation. In this section, we devote ourselves to exploring mindset thoroughly. In this particular chapter, we first define mindset, then demonstrate how it determines:

- What change leaders see and perceive in their reality;
- The quality of change leaders' internal experience;
- How much change leadership ability leaders manifest;
- Whether change leaders assume responsibility for their experience and results or whether they feel victimized by external circumstances; and
- Whether or not change leaders walk their talk.

We also discuss mindset as it relates to organizational culture. In the next chapter, we will deepen our exploration of mindset by investigating the common set of assumptions about reality that most change leaders hold, how these limit change leadership success, and how assumptions must evolve to promote successful change strategy design and implementation.

Many leaders were first introduced to the notion of mindset and how it impacts leadership performance through Joel Barker's video series on "paradigm shifts," which was based on Thomas Kuhn's ideas (1962). Then Peter Senge (1990) popularized the concepts of personal mastery and mental models in his bestseller, *The Fifth Discipline*, where he suggested that identifying one's mental models and evolving them is at the essence of personal mastery. Senge's work helped legitimize this concept for leaders and consultants and furthered the discussion of mindset in organizations. Now the discussion of mindset needs to move to center stage in leading and consulting to transformation.

Formally addressing the topic of mindset enables change leaders to ask critical questions of themselves, such as:

- How does my mindset influence my decisions, actions, and results?

- What aspects of my mindset contribute to my ability to lead transformation, and what aspects of my mindset limit my success?

- What role does my mindset play in who I am as a change leader today and in becoming the change leader I want to be?

- What beliefs and assumptions exist in my mindset that I am not even aware of, yet limit the quality of my performance and life?

Mindset is the leverage point for transforming organizations. Without initially transforming their mindsets, leaders and employees would continue to operate in their old ways, thus stifling the organization's ability to implement its new design and execute its new business strategy. Figure 4.1 graphically portrays this. Notice that the left side of the figure is the Drivers of Change Model from Chapter One, while the right side of the figure is the Drivers of Change Model in reverse. Together, they show that the need for change is *driven* from the outside in, but the outcomes of change are *caused* from the inside out. The figure shows that the results produced by transformation are initiated through breakthroughs in leader and employee mindset, which then enable each to generate and sustain new behaviors. Collectively, changes in leader and employee behavior shift the organization's culture.

Figure 4.1. Mindset: The Leverage Point for Transformation

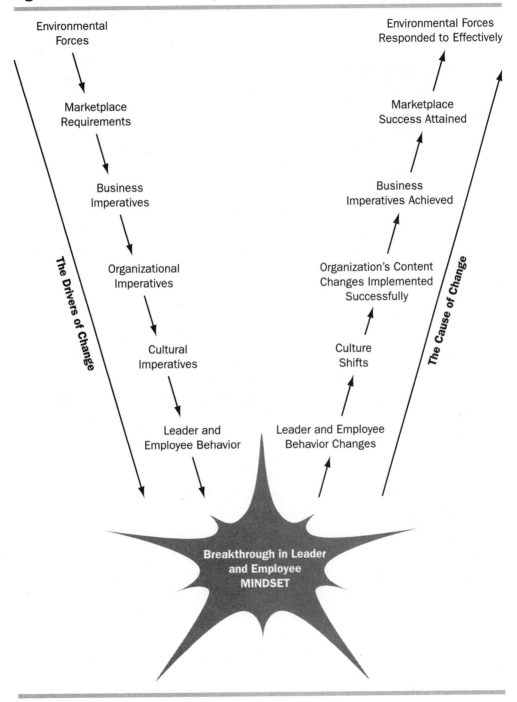

The new culture, the organization's collective new way of being, working, and relating, enables the organization's content changes (structure, systems, processes, technology) to be implemented and run successfully, which enables the organization to achieve its new business imperatives. Marketplace success is thus attained, and the originating environmental forces are responded to effectively.

The figure portrays this change in linear, cause-and-effect fashion to show the "upward" direction of primary influence. The forces of change, however, actually occur across all the variables simultaneously, with change in one variable impacting the other variables, as described in the twenty-one dimensions of conscious transformation presented in the last chapter.

What Is Mindset?

Mindset is one's worldview, the place or orientation from which you experience your reality and form your perceptions of it. The cornerstones of your mindset are your fundamental assumptions about reality and your core beliefs about self, others, and life in general. "Mental models," a phrase coined by Peter Senge and others promoting the learning organization, are similar to our definition of fundamental assumptions and core beliefs. Whatever labels you prefer, these are the core constructs of your mind that organize incoming sensory data to create *meaning* out of the sights, sounds, smells, tastes, and sensations that you experience through your interface with reality.

Mindset is comprised of a number of interdependent variables that collectively work together as one integrated system to form your worldview. While your fundamental assumptions and core beliefs form the foundation of your mindset, mindset actually includes your thoughts and attitudes, as well as your values, choices, and desires. Your needs, wants, hopes, and concerns are all a part of your mindset, as are your fears, worries, fantasies, and illusions. Together, these aspects of your mindset form the screen through which you view your world.

Mindset is different from awareness. Metaphorically, awareness is the blank canvas upon which your perception draws your reality. Mindset is the filter through which you screen what gets drawn and interpret its meaning.

Mindset is different from knowledge. Whereas knowledge can be seen as the *content* of one's mind, mindset is the mental framework that constructs a particular meaning from that content.

Mindset is also different from thinking, which can be seen as the overt *process* of your mind.[1] There are different types of thinking, such as rational thinking, strategic thinking, intuitive thinking, visual thinking, or linear thinking. No matter what type of thinking you are engaged in, mindset is the context within which all of your thinking occurs.

We also differentiate mindset from emotions and behavior. Webster defines emotions as "the affective aspect of consciousness; feeling; the state of feeling; a psychic and physical reaction subjectively experienced as strong feeling and physiologically involving changes that prepare the body for immediate vigorous action." From our perspective, emotions are the qualitative descriptors you place on the sensations caused in your body by your mindset. When your mindset perceives an event as "threatening," you experience certain associated emotions—fear, stress, anxiety, doubt, frustration, nervousness, and so forth. Some people label these emotions as negative, but we see them simply as "contracted," causing certain responses within your body to prepare you for handling a threat: muscles tighten; breath shortens; heart rate and blood pressure increase; specific hormones flood your body; and your nervous system becomes more excited. These emotions are simply your mindset's way of sounding the battle cry.

When your mindset deems an external event to be valuable or supportive, you experience "expanded" emotions—confidence, excitement, happiness, pleasure— and your body responds accordingly. Your breath gets longer and deeper; your muscles relax; and different sets of hormones are triggered. The point is that emotions are neither good nor bad; they are simply the bodily sensations attributed to certain mindsets. "E-motions" are simply the energy in motion in your body based on how you are interpreting reality at the time.

Webster defines behavior as "the manner of conducting oneself; the way in which something behaves." Behavior is not necessarily the action you do, but the tone or quality you place into action. Behavior is the bridge between the inner world of your thoughts and emotions and the outer world of your actions and results.

---

[1]There are other, more subtle processes of your mind whose descriptions go beyond the scope of this book. See Ken Wilber's books for superb discussions of these more subtle dynamics of human consciousness.

Way of Being

Mindset, emotions, and behavior are intricately linked and interact with one another as an interconnected system we refer to as one's *way of being*. For example, if leaders possess a mindset that "change should be fast and painless," when complex, long-term change is actually required, they may feel angry and frustrated at the slow pace. Behaviorally, they may become controlling, domineering, and autocratic. Their mindset, emotion, and behavior are triggered as one unified shift in their way of being.

Way of being is a powerful concept. It can be used to describe how leaders are "being" and expressing themselves at any point in time or how they are relating to others in various circumstances and situations. Because mindset causes emotions and behavior, it is the source of leaders' way of being.

People make reference to others' ways of being frequently. An example that illustrates this pertains to Sue, the senior vice president of manufacturing in one of our client organizations. When John, one of her direct reports, returned from a meeting with Sue, his team immediately asked, "How did Sue respond to our issue?" John replied, "She was responsive and concerned about fixing the problem." John's answer revealed Sue's "content" position about the problem, while simultaneously alluding to Sue's way of being.

In our change leadership coaching practice, we often ask change leaders to make clear distinctions between their ways of being and what they do—their actions. Usually, leaders focus primarily on what they do and pay little attention to how they are coming across to others; they focus only on the external world at the expense of their internal world. This creates numerous problems. For example, when leaders take action, they assume they will have a certain impact or produce a specific outcome. However, taking action with different ways of being can create very different results. In the above example, if Sue had been defensive and hostile, even though she may have ultimately agreed to resolve the team's problem, her confrontational way of being would have had a much different impact on the team than if she had been positive and genuinely concerned. Way of being is a powerful force in human interaction.

We also find it very beneficial to help change leaders differentiate among their mindsets, emotions, and behavior. This provides them with greater self-awareness and deeper insight into the dynamics and patterns of their ways of being. Because each can be accessed for alteration and improvement using different Self Mastery tools, differentiating among mindset, emotions, and behaviors enables conscious leaders to more easily unravel and transform the leadership styles that limit their effectiveness in leading transformation. As in tuning an engine, it helps to know the different roles and functions of the carburetor, spark plugs, and fuel pump so you can use the proper tools for each. By becoming consciously aware of their habitual ways of being, change leaders can greatly improve their impact.

The Impact of Mindset on Perception

Most leaders, regardless of who they are or where they come from, often confuse the events that happen with their mental constructs of those events. The two are so intricately woven that leaders often do not realize the impact their mindsets have on determining their perceptions of reality. Because reality and perception are so seamlessly intertwined, people don't see that they are in fact two distinct phenomena. They make the mistake of assuming that their perception of reality is objective, when it seldom is.

Figure 4.2 demonstrates this dynamic. What you perceive in reality is influenced by your mindset, just as your mindset determines your experience of what you perceive. Notice the two-way relationship; mindset influences what you perceive "out there" and what you experience "in here." Therefore, mindset impacts both your external reality and your internal reality. This will become more clear as we proceed.

Figure 4.2. The Seamless Connection Between Mindset and Reality

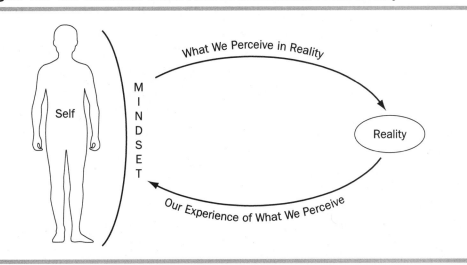

Leaders' mental constructions of reality often cause them to see a world that doesn't really exist. Mindset is extremely powerful; it can construct whatever "objective" reality leaders want to believe in. People once thought that the world was flat. This belief did not make the world flat. It did not change the empirical evidence. It simply determined the meaning that was made of the empirical evidence and caused people to act as if the world were flat.

Because of this seamless connection between reality and mindset, it is very difficult to know what is reality and what is interpretation or a mental construct of reality. Is the world flat, or do you just see it as flat? Are your employees resistant, or do you just see them that way?

The observer and the observed are deeply interconnected. Change leaders who approach transformation *reactively* consistently slip into the delusion that reality and their interpretation of it are one and the same. Because they do not see and understand the difference between reality and mindset, they cannot strategically address how mindset influences perception, either their own or anyone else's. Consequently, mindset—the most powerful of change levers in all human systems, from individuals to societies—goes unattended. Confusing reality and their interpretation of reality is one of the most debilitating errors reactive change leaders make; it often causes them to perceive their transformation inaccurately. We will illustrate the profound impact of mindset on what change leaders perceive in their change efforts when we explore fundamental assumptions in the next chapter.

Conscious leaders, because they have explored their own internal dynamics, are aware of the influence of mindset on perception and consider it in every critical decision or action they take. Because they realize that mindset influences their own and others' perceptions, conscious leaders ensure that they and others explore their mindsets as a central strategy of their organization's transformation process. They assess the mental models that influence their assessment of data, their design decisions, and their implementation plans. Addressing the influence of mindset on perception enables conscious leaders to optimize both their internal experience and decision making and their external end results. Let's now look more deeply into how mindset influences change leaders' internal states of being.

The Impact of Mindset on State of Being

The reticular activating system (RAS), which lies at the base of the brain stem, is among the most primitive parts of the brain, sometimes referred to as the "reptilian brain." The RAS is the gateway for incoming sensory information, sending it to either the conscious mind or the subconscious mind (see Figure 4.3).

Figure 4.3. Reticular Activating System

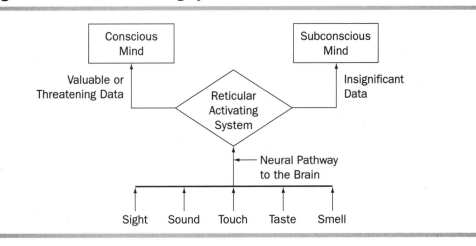

The RAS sends both valuable and threatening information to the *conscious* mind; you then become aware of it and can respond appropriately. The RAS sends information that is neither valuable nor threatening to the *subconscious* mind. Because this information is insignificant, the RAS does not bother you with it. Because you are not made aware of this information, you do not know it is being input into your brain. It simply is recorded as an unconscious memory (Penfield, 1975).

What tells the RAS how to process the information you receive about external events? What determines whether the incoming data is perceived as valuable, threatening, or inconsequential? Your neo-cortex does—the programming and conditioning of your mindset!

For example, events happen: The stock market goes up; your customer service rating goes down; your biggest client orders $10M worth of product; your idea is rejected in the staff meeting; your child's soccer team wins the tournament; your mortgage check bounces. Some events you label as "good," and you react favorably to them. Other events you label as "bad," and you react negatively to those. Your reaction is determined by your mindset or how you perceive and judge what you experience. It is not determined by the event itself.

Most people believe that events in reality have inherent value. In other words, some things are positive while others are negative. However, most of reality is comprised of "neutral" events, which are not good or bad in themselves. They just are. You register these neutral events through your senses of sight, sound, taste, smell, and touch.[2] Your mindset then adds meaning to these events, evaluating them as either valuable, threatening, or insignificant. The "valuable" data triggers an "expanded" state of being; the "threatening" data triggers a "contracted" internal state; and the "insignificant" data produces no reaction at all. Specific information, valued or feared by your mindset, then becomes the trigger of an expanded or contracted emotional and behavioral response within you. Your state of being, moment by moment, is thus determined by your mindset. The *source of your reaction, whether it be positive or negative, is the meaning made by your mindset.*

A great example of the influence of mindset on the perception of reality and resulting internal reaction occurred to us in 1991 when our home and office burned to the ground. We *saw* the same flames, *heard* the same crackling and crashing sounds, *smelled* the same smoke, *felt* the same heat, *tasted* the same smoky taste. Dean "constructed" the sensory data he received into an experience of joyful freedom—being released from the burden of having too many possessions. With the same information, Linda constructed an experience of grief and sadness at the loss of the precious symbols of her life and history. Neither of our experiences was better or worse than the other or more right or wrong. Our experiences were simply different—drastically different.

The information our senses brought to each of us was processed and perceived through very different mindsets. Dean values freedom and simplicity; Linda values a relationship to her cherished surroundings, beauty, and comfort. Both value systems are equally legitimate, yet created profoundly different responses to the same fire.

To summarize our discussion of mindset so far, we *believe* that objective reality exists, yet people see different realities and construct various meanings about those realities through their unique mindsets. People don't always see what is actually "out there," and what they think they see determines their internal state of being. Conscious leaders, then, must always reflect on and test their thoughts and assumptions about reality, rather than unconsciously assume reality to be what they think it is.

---

[2]In this explanation, we are using a mechanical description of brain functioning to simplify our point. Please note, however, that current brain/mind research reveals a much more complex and holistic functioning of the brain (see Grof, 1993; Pribram, 1971).

The Fundamental Law of Success

Mindset not only influences change leaders' perception and internal experience, but also their external performance and results. A very simple equation called the Fundamental Law of Success (Anderson, 1988) clearly demonstrates the impact of mindset on performance. This law is stated as

$$\text{Ability Level} \times \text{Mental State} = \text{Performance}$$

Your ability level establishes your *potential* for success. It is a product of your experience, training, and genetics. Ability increases or decreases based on your practice routine, but at any point in time, you have a distinct ability level.

Ability does not guarantee success. Ask any athlete. Sometimes the most skilled athlete loses, or the lesser skilled wins. Herein lies the impact of mindset on performance. Mindset, which directly influences the inner state you are in when you are performing (or at any other time, for that matter), determines how much of your potential you actualize.

As Table 4.1 illustrates, if you are 100 percent focused, then you perform at 100 percent of your ability level. You reach your potential because you are fully present and engaged, in the "flow" or the "zone," as many high performers describe it. However, if you are distracted or preoccupied, then your performance suffers because you are performing at less than 100 percent. If 20 percent of your mindset

Table 4.1. Fundamental Law of Success

		Ability Level	Mental State	Performance
Person B	Trial 1	10	100% Focus	10
	Trial 2	10	80% Focus	8
	Trial 3	10	60% Focus	6
Person A	Trial 1	8	60% Focus	4.8
	Trial 2	8	80% Focus	6.4
	Trial 3	8	100% Focus	8

is occupied elsewhere, then only 80 percent of your ability can manifest. You under-perform by the 20 percent that is engaged elsewhere. This phenomenon is true whether you are leading transformation, playing golf, or nurturing your children.

People tend to perform best when they are confident, calm, and centered because that "expanded" state of being makes it easier to focus 100 percent on the task. When people are in a "contracted" state—experiencing fear, doubt, or anxiety—they tend to lose focus because they are mentally and emotionally preoccupied with their internal upset. However, the best performers in any discipline, from sports to acting to leading transformation, are those people who have developed the ability to manage their internal state and can maintain 100 percent focus on the task, regardless of their emotions. For these "masterful" people, contracted emotions don't distract them.

In Table 4.1, notice how Person A's performance suffers as he loses mental focus over the three trials. See how Person B's performance improves as she increases her focus over the three trials. Notice also that a lesser skilled person can actually perform better than a person of greater skill—if the lesser skilled person is in a more "centered" and "focused" state of mind.

The Fundamental Law of Success is true for all levels of human systems—individuals, teams, organizations, and societies. At the organizational level, we speak of culture and core competencies instead of talking about mindset and performance, but the outcome is the same. Assume two companies have similar missions, core competencies, strategies, staffs, and skills. One possesses a culture that is vibrant, results-oriented, "can-do," information-sharing, learning-oriented, and passionate about serving customers. The other company's culture is staid and static, based on entitlement, risk aversion, information hoarding, and an attitude of "we know what is best for the customer." Whose stock are you going to buy? Clearly, the organization whose culture unleashes its people's potential will win every time, as long as they possess and apply capability near commensurate with their competitors. Like mindset, culture determines how much of the organization's potential for success is achieved.

Self Mastery

As the Fundamental Law of Success indicates, transforming mindset is the most direct way to achieve more of one's potential. *Self Mastery* is the practice by which high-performing change leaders optimize their mindsets and ways of being. The central principle of Self Mastery is that *mindset is causative,* that change leaders' internal state of being influences the results they can create.

The Self Mastery Model (shown in Figure 4.4) shows how mindset impacts change leaders' results. Notice that the model illustrates the two-way relationship between mindset and reality that we discussed earlier. Let's go through the model step by step.

Figure 4.4. The Self Mastery Model

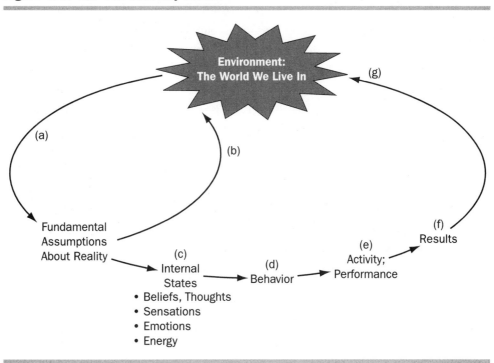

There is a two-way relationship between the external environment and leaders' fundamental assumptions about reality—events happen in the external environment and they influence and affect leaders' fundamental assumptions about reality (a) and, once formed, leaders' fundamental assumptions about reality also determine what they see in reality (b). The interface between leaders' fundamental assumptions about reality and what actually happens in reality (objective facts) "causes" their internal state—their beliefs, thoughts, sensations, emotions, and energy (c). Leaders' internal states then determine their behavior and way of being, the manner in which they conduct themselves (d). Their behavior and way of being in turn shape their actions and performance (e), which impact their results (f). Leaders' results then become a part of their external environment (g), and the process continues as they perceive their new reality.

The Self Mastery Model shows us that the results we create are rooted in our mindset and way of being. Everything—your attitude, feelings, behavior, actions, and results—stems from your mindset. This does not mean, as some theorists might suggest, that altering your mindset automatically produces a concomitant shift in results. You still have to deal with the forces of the external world and the need to *do* something. Believing you can fly does not mean that you can fly. However, transforming your mindset does increase the probability of success because an optimal state of mind enables you to manifest more of your ability as you engage in the actions required to produce your desired outcome.

Change leaders can *internally* influence their external reality through greater Self Mastery in two ways. First, they can be more focused and centered as they perform. This requires *self-management skill,* the ability to manage one's internal state of being in *real time* to generate maximum focus and a desired way of being. Second, they can overcome historical or conditioned fears, doubts, and self-limiting ways of being that either keep them from being fully focused in present time or cause undesirable behaviors. This requires *personal transformation skill,* a process that takes place *over time.*

Notice the relationship between self-management and personal transformation. Self-management is what change leaders do "online" to adjust their internal state during real-time activities to maximize their performance. Personal transformation is what change leaders do "off-line" over time to prepare themselves for optimal online performance. It is how they overcome habitual reactions so they won't need to adjust them in real time. Both of these skills begin with conscious awareness and a strong inner witnessing capability.

When change leaders are operating "unconsciously," they have no ability to adjust their internal state; the quality of their internal state occurs automatically and reflects their conditioned response at that moment. When change leaders are operating "consciously" and are able to witness themselves in action, they have the opportunity to observe and course correct their internal state to intentionally produce one that will better support their outcomes.

There are a number of Self Mastery processes, tools, and techniques that change leaders can use to improve both their self-management and personal transformation skills. These include the following:

- Breathing techniques;

- Body awareness and relaxation techniques;

- Mental rehearsal tools, including visualization and affirmations;

- Emotional release techniques;

- Focusing techniques;

- Behavior pattern reprogramming;

- Personal visioning and purpose identification;

- Energy management;

- Diet and exercise;

- Values clarification;

- Core belief identification; and

- Behavioral style assessments.

This list is by no means complete, but it does attend to all four domains of human experience: physical, emotional, mental, and spiritual—which any effective self-mastery approach must do.

The key to Self Mastery, like with any skill set, is *practice.* The processes, tools, and techniques listed above are only effective if they are used regularly. In our change leadership development work, we consistently see that those change leaders who establish and maintain a daily practice of Self Mastery become the most masterful change leaders. No ifs, ands, or buts. Practice makes perfect.

Committing to a daily practice of Self Mastery is a natural by-product of choosing to live and lead transformation consciously. In fact, Self Mastery begins with your choice to turn inward—to reflect about who you are and how you are in the world.

Let's illustrate the power of consciously pursuing Self Mastery through an example of two change leaders who were co-workers in a manufacturing plant we worked with.

▶ CASE ɪɴ POINT

Our role in this intervention was to help the executive team transform the plant from "worst-in-class" to "best-in-class." Early in the change effort, Henry, the team leader, committed himself to pursing his own Self Mastery with our assistance. Henry was the new facility manager, a young upstart recently out of business school who thought he knew all the latest management approaches to improving work processes. Joe was the production superintendent of the facility, a hard-nosed, long-term employee with twenty years of service who was the technical expert in running the manufacturing facility's machinery. Both Henry and Joe were loyal employees who wanted to contribute the most they could to the organization.

Joe, who represented the "old guard," resisted Henry's new ideas and refused to implement them fully. Henry felt threatened by Joe's resistance, for he realized that the entire facility was swayed by Joe's opinions. For three months, Henry and Joe went at it toe-to-toe, with no resolution in sight. As a result of their constant bickering, the plant's executive team was in disarray, divided along party lines between the "newcomers" and the "old guard." The plant's performance continued to deteriorate, primarily as a result of the leaders being unable to agree to a change strategy.

Henry, in exasperation, requested some coaching from us. We taught him a number of Self Mastery tools, which he began to practice and apply effectively. As a result, he began to explore his fundamental assumptions and core beliefs about the situation. With some assistance, Henry began to realize that he was assuming that Joe was a threat, perceiving Joe as inherently obstinate, and battling with Joe from the belief that if he, Henry, didn't "win," he would lose face and credibility with the other managers. Looking deeper within himself, Henry saw that his hostility toward Joe was driven by his own desire and need to be seen as competent, which he saw as his path to being included and liked by the other leaders. Henry realized that this competency issue came from his own deep-seated doubt in himself and his desire to make a real contribution. When he wasn't sure that he was capable, Henry usually felt that others saw him as incapable, and that frightened him because he had such a high need to be included and liked.

Henry's new awareness of his previously unconscious mindset enabled him to begin a personal transformation process. He began to acknowledge his own competence separate from what others thought of him and began to view Joe as an ally who held the shared vision of making the facility as successful as possible. This shift of mindset, along with breathing and centering techniques, enabled Henry to *behave* and *act* differently toward

Joe in real time. Rather than tell Joe how his old ways were wrong, Henry began to listen to Joe more, to entertain Joe's views rather than pontificate his own. Over the course of a few weeks, Henry's change in behavior and performance began to alter his *results* with Joe. Joe began to tone down his own hostility toward Henry; Joe had less reason to fight because Henry was no longer his adversary. Soon Joe began to listen more himself and was surprised by the good ideas he heard coming from Henry. As Joe warmed to Henry's innovations, he tried a few of them, and their successes helped Joe build further trust in Henry.

Over time, Henry and Joe's bond strengthened as the performance of the facility improved. The rest of the management staff began to temper their own hostilities as they saw their leaders cooperate more. Soon they had a collaborative solution for transforming the facility. In the end, Henry and Joe formed a tight partnership based on mutual respect and open acknowledgement that each brought different and equally essential pieces of the facility's overall formula for success. The team excelled, and the plant emerged twelve months later to become "best-in-class." ◄

This case demonstrates the importance of Self Mastery in action and its ability to help change leaders recognize and change their mindsets and behavior through both self-management and personal transformation processes and tools. The story illustrates the basic behavioral tenet of Self Mastery: *Fix yourself first, then others and the environment will follow.* When you "fix" your own mindset first and then return to a clear and centered internal state, you are better able to deal with the situation you face. In Henry's case, he was able to create a powerful partnership with Joe because he saw how his own mindset was creating the hostile relationship with Joe. He owned that he was responsible for contributing to their conflict. Yes, bull-headed Joe also contributed, but Henry realized that he could not change Joe. He could only change himself. Consequently, he "woke" to his previously unconscious mindset and antagonistic way of behaving toward Joe and altered himself accordingly. When he shifted his mindset about Joe, his feelings, behavior, and actions began to change. Because he was relating to Joe in a different way, the set up a different dynamic between them. Over time, these new conditions between Henry and Joe enabled Joe and the rest of the management staff to alter their own mindsets and behavior. Henry modeled the fundamental way of being of a conscious change leader. He fixed himself first, which set up the conditions for the others to evolve to a more productive way of operating together.

Change leaders' capabilities expand the moment they realize that the leverage point for transforming external events (their organization) is transforming their own internal mindset about those events. When change leaders take responsibility for the self-generated constructs of their own limiting mindset and transform them, they acquire the potential to relate to the external situation in a way that enables the situation to change. It is difficult for change leaders to see a solution to a change-related problem without first altering their mindset. Albert Einstein said it best in his now-famous quote: "The problems that exist in the world today cannot be solved by the level of thinking that created them." To solve or change anything of significance, change leaders must first transform their mindset. Pursuing Self Mastery unleashes this capability.

Awareness: The Foundation of Self Mastery

Greater Self Mastery begins with becoming consciously aware of which of our ways of being generate desired results and which cause unwanted outcomes. Change leaders who have this awareness are equipped to catch their self-limiting mental, emotional, and behavioral patterns before they negatively influence critical change activities. Plus, knowing their effective internal states gives them a better chance of intentionally producing them, especially during important planning sessions or design meetings.

Exhibit 4.1 offers a worksheet that can increase your awareness of your own effective and ineffective ways of being. Use it as a real-time log to record your experience. Fill it in as soon as possible after leaving situations in which you were either very "centered" and effective or in which you reacted negatively in ways you would like to change. Describe what occurred in the situation that "triggered" your positive or negative reaction. Be as specific as you can, especially about your physical sensations, emotions, and internal "self-talk." As you become familiar with both your self-limiting and excellence-producing internal states, you will discern them more quickly so you can either course correct or reinforce them. Over time, your physical sensations and thoughts will become wake-up calls that activate your inner witness for real-time self-management and off-line personal transformation work.

Exhibit 4.1. Assessing Your Way of Being

External Situation	Emotional Response	Physical Sensations	Thoughts, Beliefs	Behaviors	Actions	Results

From Victim to Full Contributor

For many change leaders, the fact that they create their own experience of reality based on how they see the world is difficult to accept, for it means that they are responsible for their own reactions, behavior, and results. It is much easier for them to assume that they are not responsible, that they are somehow a victim of the external forces around them. The belief pattern of this victim mentality goes something like this: "Events happen and they affect me; I cannot control how I feel or react. The events cause me to feel and behave the way I do." This victim mindset results from not distinguishing the influence of mindset on one's perception of reality, which is where we started this discussion.

Change leaders' reactive, victimized worldview sets up the conditions for their failure, which is often the price they pay for being unconscious of the fact that external events and their perceptions of them are two distinct phenomena. Initially, in their relationship, Henry and Joe held onto this victim mentality, blaming one another for their conflict. This worldview is the common way of being for most people, most of the time. Most people are not aware of the extent to which they are giving up their personal power to change and to create the results they want. They focus more on complaining about why the organization or other people are not allowing them to succeed. Change leaders, above all others, must not fall into this victim mindset, but must model self-responsibility to the organization.

Although change leaders may not be able to change certain external events in their transformation efforts, they can change how they perceive and react to them. They can then shift their personal experience of the events and raise the probability of having a more positive impact. This process, the heart of Self Mastery, enables change leaders to become full contributors to their situations, adding energy and value.

Embracing the fact that you significantly influence your results and the quality of your life based on your mindset and way of being can be both liberating and terrifying. It is liberating to recognize your own self-imposed limitations and to choose new and more effective ways of being, relating, and working. However, this can be terrifying as you face the fact that you are much more powerful and capable than you ever imagined. As Marianne Williamson (1992) wrote, "Our deepest fear is not that we are inadequate. Our deepest fear is that we are powerful beyond measure. It is our light, not our darkness, that most frightens us." Placing your attention on the real source of change—yourself—enables you to become more powerful, more able to contribute to your organization's transformation in profound ways.

Walking the Talk of Change

The most important change leadership role is for leaders to walk the talk of the change, to model the transformation they are after in the organization. Leaders saying one thing and doing another is a path to certain failure. It breeds distrust and dissention, increases employee resistance, and damages all hopes of building employee commitment for the transformation.

Change leaders' ability to walk the talk of change comes from a sustained focus and commitment to their own Self Mastery process. Walking the talk, by definition, requires personal growth and change. The "talk" denotes the vision, the ideal or desired state. The "walk" denotes current behaviors and actions. If leaders always behaved and acted as their vision suggests, then change would not be necessary. But change is necessary, because, like everyone, they make mistakes as they strive toward their ideal. There are times when change leaders do walk their talk and times when they don't. Therefore, becoming aware of how they are being and what impact it is having on others and then correcting their course is key.

Walking your talk does not mean that you need to be consistent or perfect all the time. Mistakes are permitted as long as you do two things—acknowledge the incongruent behavior and make overt amends for it and become more consistent in your talk and walk over time. Both require you to be consciously aware of your mindset and behavior in real time and to use Self Mastery skills and techniques to change your mindset and behavior as needed.

It is relatively easy for people to break a behavioral habit in an isolated situation, but far more difficult for them to sustain the new behavior over time. This was Henry's greatest challenge in the earlier case. Whenever differences of opinion grew heated between Henry and Joe, Henry had to maintain conscious awareness of his mindset and behavior. Otherwise, he would slip back into unconsciously trying to win the battle with Joe to demonstrate his competence. We had numerous coaching sessions with Henry, helping him to unwind this deep-rooted reactive tendency. The Self Mastery tools we taught Henry—core belief identification, body relaxation, breathing and centering techniques, mental imagery, and affirmations—enabled him to sustain his conscious awareness and alter his behavior when under stress. Henry didn't walk his talk every time. However, he did walk his talk over time, which impacted Joe significantly.

Self Mastery is critical to successful change leadership. Our challenge has been to demonstrate that these notions and practices are more than good ideas; for transformational change leaders, they are *essential*. As unpracticed concepts, however, they are not worth much more than the paper they are written on. Self-management and personal transformation skills can only be developed through regular practice.

Let's turn now to address organizational culture. First, we will define culture, then address the role Self Mastery plays in transforming culture.

Culture and Mindset

Culture is to organizations as mindset is to individuals. Culture is the sum of all the individual mindsets rolled into one set of common agreements. Within culture lies the company's core values, its norms and operating principles, its myths and stories. Culture is the way of being of the organization, exerting influence over people's morale and spirit. It determines what types of individual behaviors are acceptable or not and shapes the behaviors and style exhibited by the organization in the marketplace. Culture is the organization's character.

Culture is initially formed as the organization takes on the mindset, behavior, and style of its founders. It is embedded over time into the very fabric of the organization through its formal and informal policies and procedures, methods, practices, and ways of operating. The leaders, overtly or not, ensure that their own worldviews, beliefs, values, and work ethic are infused into how the organization operates. Think about Watson at IBM, Hewlett and Packard in their company, Debbie Fields in Mrs. Field's Cookies, or Ben and Jerry. These leaders put their own cultural mark on their organization while it was in its early, formative stages. There is nothing wrong with this; it is just what happens when people organize and work together over a period of time. Culture forms whether we want it to or not. The only variable is what it forms into. In the field of organization development, we talk of "indicators of culture" such as:

- Leadership style;

- Communication patterns;

- Decision-making styles;

- Use of information;

- Use of electronic communication as a vehicle for information sharing, decision making, and relationship building;

- Level classifications and privileges;

- Performance standards and expectations;

- Consequences of failure;

- Space/layout;

- Norms and behavior;

- Stories, myths, traditions, and rituals;

- Heroes and heroines; and

- Symbols (brand, logo, motto, language, relics).

We call these indicators of culture because they make the culture overt. They are the signposts of culture, the tell-tales that collectively reveal the personality of the organization. Behind each indicator is a mindset, a shared agreement about a certain belief, value, or way of seeing the world. For example, organizations that possess the norm of placing severe limitations on mid-manager's spending authority often carry the belief that people can't be trusted or that top-down control is essential to business success. The spending restriction is simply the indicator of the given belief in action.

Seasoned change consultants can very quickly and accurately assess the basic culture of any organization by gathering information about a handful of these key indicators. For example, assume an organization has numerous levels of hierarchy with strictly enforced privilege policies, like who parks his or her car where or who gets what size office. Also assume that in this organization, information is protected and closely held as a sign of power, and that when information is shared it flows generally from top to bottom in the form of announcements about corporate policy decisions. Assume also that the highest ranking person in a meeting makes all of the decisions, that mistakes are punished heavily, and that no formal structure or process for learning or feedback exists.

Given these indicators, what is the culture of this organization? You can safely bet that this is a "power and control" culture in which rank delivers significant privilege and authority, leaders solicit little employee input and make all key decisions, employees are disempowered and reactive, and people "cover their butts" rather than take risks. You might expect the organization to be highly unionized, with poor customer service ratings and a traumatic track record of change. Certainly you would have to dig a bit deeper to check out these assumptions, but these few key indicators would likely give you a fairly accurate first assessment of the culture and its underlying mindset.

Transforming culture is a central aspect of virtually all organization-wide transformation efforts. Remember that transformation entails "content" changes that are so profound that they require people's "collective way of being, working, and relating" (culture) to transform to implement and sustain them. Traditional, top-down, command-and-control cultures, for the most part, cannot successfully deliver the fast-paced technological, consumer-focused, relationship-based, whole-system-oriented content changes required by today's marketplace.

Attention to culture is a make-or-break factor in successful transformation. We have seen numerous examples of organizations spending millions of dollars on information technology installations, only to have the old cultural norms stifle the implementation and subsequent use of the technology. The investment was made, the technology installed, but the people did not use it and the potential benefits were lost.

Shifting culture so that it matches the needs of the organization in the future must be overtly addressed in all transformational change strategies. Culture change requires interventions at all levels of organization—whole system, team, relationships, and individuals. All must be aligned with the new directions and serve the content changes being made. Leaders can use organization-wide interventions such as visioning, values clarification, breakthrough and Self Mastery training, governance, corporate policy, communications processes, and human resources practices (for example, succession planning, hiring practices, pay systems, and performance management systems).

Leaders can affect the culture of work groups and teams through clarifying team vision and values, roles and responsibility, communications patterns, operating norms, decision making, team learning, recognition, and compensation. At the relationship level, leaders can influence culture by modeling and encouraging relationship contracting, giving and receiving feedback effectively, negotiating roles and responsibilities, clarifying interpersonal behavioral patterns, managing conflict, and determining mutual accountabilities. Individually, their cultural interventions can focus on personal behaviors, such as being responsible for one's actions, honoring commitments, developing emotional intelligence, telling the truth, owning mistakes, learning, and producing results on time and on budget. However, some of the most powerful and direct cultural interventions place Self Mastery as the foundation of effective relationship, team, and whole-system interventions. From our perspective, Self Mastery should be the cornerstone of most culture transformations.

All cultural interventions, no matter what the level of human system change leaders are addressing, begin and end with mindset. If the leaders are working at the organization level, then they must consider and address the collective mindset and include it in their change strategies. When addressing team issues, they must include a strategy for discussing and influencing the group's mindset, and so forth. Strategies such as training and communications are essential, but they will be insufficient without a direct focus on culture and mindset.

Summary

In this chapter, we have demonstrated that mindset is causative, that the mindsets change leaders hold influence: (1) What they see in their transformations; (2) their internal experiences; and (3) their performance and results. We showed that the significant impact of mindset calls for the ongoing pursuit of Self Mastery and that learning and practicing self-management and personal transformation processes are critical. We also demonstrated how cultural transformation must be supported by personal transformation.

In the next chapter, we will deepen our exploration of mindset by exploring the impact of change leaders' fundamental assumptions about reality on their success.

Over the years, we have discovered that the most competent change leaders all possess one common trait: They continually question and explore their fundamental assumptions, seeking deeper clarification of what's true in reality, rather than assuming that they already know. They strive to be conscious of their fundamental assumptions and beliefs about reality so they won't inadvertently reach inaccurate conclusions. There are many now-famous conclusions that were subsequently found to be false, such as, "The world is flat" and "Humans will never fly."

As an introduction to the next chapter, we leave you with some of our favorite mistaken "certainties":

> "This 'telephone' has too many shortcomings to be seriously considered
> as a means of communication. The device is inherently of no value to us."
> —*Western Union internal memo, 1876*

> "The wireless music box has no imaginable commercial value. Who would
> pay for a message sent to nobody in particular?"
> —*David Sarnoff's associates in response to his urgings*
> *for investments in the radio in the 1920s*

"We don't like their sound, and guitar music is on the way out."
> —*Decca Recording Company, rejecting the Beatles, 1962*

"There is no reason anyone would want a computer in their home."
> —*Ken Olson, president, chairman, and founder*
> *of Digital Equipment Corporation, 1977*

"Drill for oil? You mean drill into the ground to try and find oil? You're crazy."
> —*Drillers whom Edwin L. Drake tried to enlist*
> *to his project to drill for oil in 1859*

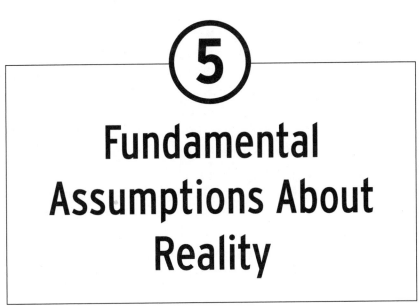

Fundamental Assumptions About Reality

A **NUMBER OF YEARS AGO,** a university professor conducted an experiment in his Introduction to Psychology class. The class was held in a large auditorium with over three hundred students present. As the professor was standing at his lectern on the stage, a large man ran aggressively toward him. The man was tall and burly and was dressed in black leather pants and a pair of black motorcycle boots. His dark hair was long and greasy, and he sported a black stocking cap pulled low over his brow. He wore large chains that dangled from both his belt loops and his boots.

As the man reached the professor, he withdrew something from underneath his jacket. The crowd gasped as the man pointed the object at the professor's chest. Simultaneously, a teaching assistant, who was hidden behind the stage curtain, fired a 22-caliber pistol loaded with blank cartridges. The students screamed and ran as the professor fell to the stage floor, and the man escaped offstage.

From behind the stage, the teaching assistant spoke over the loudspeaker to bring calm to the class, "The professor is all right. This is a simulation. Please calm down and return to your seats."

The professor stood and asked the class, "What did you just see occur?" The majority of the class reported that they saw a hoodlum shoot the professor with a large caliber pistol. Why do you think they saw a pistol, when in fact, the man was wielding a large yellow banana?

The majority of students saw a false reality because of their mindset and the erroneous assumption it formulated from the data they had. Their mindsets constructed the sights and sounds to mean "hoodlum" and "murder." They reacted to dynamics that weren't actually there. This happens all too often in transformation.

Leaders must accurately perceive the dynamics of transformation to be able to formulate an optimal change strategy. We believe that most transformational change efforts fail because the change leaders inadvertently make erroneous assumptions about what is happening in their change initiatives. They make these incorrect assumptions because their deeply held mental model of reality, or what we call their *fundamental assumption* about reality, is, in fact, inaccurate. These false fundamental assumptions about reality then influence the change leaders' beliefs about organizations, people, and change, causing them to perceive a set of dynamics that are different from the ones that actually exist. Consequently, these leaders respond to their misperceptions by building a change strategy that is ill-suited for the transformational reality they face. Most of the previously discussed common problems with leading transformation stem from these erroneous fundamental assumptions.

This chapter explores two very different sets of fundamental assumptions about reality that have direct and substantial impact on the success of change leadership. We call these the *Industrial Mindset* and the *Emerging Mindset.* Research in various sciences, such as physics, biology, and chemistry, is demonstrating that a number of modern society's socially accepted fundamental assumptions about reality (the Industrial Mindset) are inaccurate. The world we live in is not the world we thought we lived in. A new understanding about reality is emerging. This new understanding is not arbitrary or based on researchers' ideas of a better worldview; it is based on sound and solid scientific *evidence.*

The science that initiated this new paradigm of understanding, quantum physics, was born over seventy years ago. Breakthroughs in chemistry, biology, and chaos theory have helped formulate the Emerging Mindset and have increased its credibility over the past thirty years. This worldview is beginning to migrate from the fringes of science into the mainstream of society.

Even though the Emerging Mindset is only beginning to show up in society's way of thinking, it is having sometimes significant impact on our social systems, such as government, education, health care, and the legal system. Examples include: (1) The public's growing disdain for bipartisanship in politics; (2) the attempt to provide more varied modes of learning in schools; (3) the move toward universal health care; and (4) the attempt to prevent crimes, not just punish them. Alone, any one of these examples is minor, yet taken together, they begin to reveal a new pattern of social thought. This will become more evident as we proceed.

The general population hardly notices the Emerging Mindset and continues to operate in the old "industrial" ways. In fact, most organizational leaders continue to lead both their current operations and their change efforts based on the old paradigm of the Industrial Mindset, which is at the root of the reactive approach to transformation discussed earlier. You cannot successfully lead transformation from the worldview of the Industrial Mindset; to succeed, you must approach transformation from the worldview of the Emerging Mindset.

In the last chapter, we saw that mindset is causative; it dramatically impacts the level of performance and results that leaders are able to achieve in transformation. In this chapter, we will deepen our understanding of mindset by exploring the most prevalent fundamental assumptions leaders hold about people, organizations, and transformation; where these assumptions come from; the influence society has had on forming these assumptions; and how many of these assumptions are inaccurate maps of reality. Most importantly, we will describe the Emerging Mindset that change leaders need to adopt to lead transformation successfully. We will conclude the chapter by identifying the ten operating principles for conscious transformation and the implications of each principle on change leadership practices.

Our Assumptions About Assumptions

Before we enter this discussion, we would like to make clear a few of our own assumptions that influence the ideas presented in this chapter:

1. We assume that objective reality exists, that reality possesses inherent dynamics that are influenced by specific laws and principles.

2. We assume that, throughout history, societies have made assumptions about objective reality based on their understanding and that these have determined their behaviors and practices.

3. We assume that some of society's assumptions have been erroneous. For example, at one time in history, people believed that the world was flat and that the earth was the center of the universe.

4. We assume that such erroneous assumptions do not change the actual nature of reality; believing the world is flat does not make it flat.

5. We assume that people's fundamental assumptions about reality, accurate or not, "construct" the reality they experience. In other words, people's assumptions do alter their subjective experience of objective reality, as well as their behavior and results. If people think the world is flat, then it is, *for them.* Consequently, assumptions about reality are critical.

6. We assume that, as science advances, some of its discoveries reveal new facts, while others simply generate new interpretations. These discoveries and the meaning applied to them, for the most part, should be treated as "assumptions," because it is often difficult to be *sure* whether something is fact or interpretation. So, while at any point in history, many of society's current assumptions about the nature of reality are its best guesses, they are still, in fact, guesses.

Consequently, we believe that understanding your current fundamental assumptions about reality and continually evolving them to be as accurate as possible gives you the greatest potential for improving your performance and results in leading transformation.

We are not suggesting that the Emerging Mindset that is being formulated at the leading edge of contemporary science is the correct and accurate view of reality, the final answer to the ancient inquiry into the fundamental nature of reality. It is not, nor can it be. We assume that human understanding will evolve over the next two hundred years, as it has evolved over the past two hundred. *However, we believe that the Emerging Mindset is clearly the next evolution in our collective understanding of the objective reality in which we live and, therefore, the doorway to the next breakthrough in all human pursuits, including leading transformation.*

Take This Chapter to Heart

Identifying the fundamental assumptions that govern your worldview is a challenging undertaking, because fundamental assumptions about reality usually reside outside of conscious awareness. We invite you to use the material in this chapter actively to discover your own fundamental assumptions. Throughout the chapter, ask yourself, "What do I believe is true about reality? Where did these beliefs come from? Am I fixed in these beliefs or am I open to other possibilities?" Your answers to these questions may catalyze new insights for you that could very well create a breakthrough in your approach to leading or consulting to transformation.

A word of caution to pragmatic and results-oriented readers: You may find this discussion too conceptual for your taste and may be tempted to skip over it. We urge you to persevere with reading this chapter, for in this chapter resides what we have come to believe is a *most critical concept for change leadership success.* In fact, your ability to apply the pragmatic tools, techniques, and change process methodology that we offer in the companion volume, *The Change Leader's Roadmap,* will be enhanced by the understanding you will develop by reading this chapter. Surfacing your basic assumptions about reality will enable you to *choose your mindset consciously* and therefore change the screen through which you perceive organizations, people, and change.

The Source of Your Fundamental Assumptions About Reality

Where did your basic assumptions about reality originate? They came from one of four sources: (1) The social constructs of society; (2) your family system; (3) your community (friends, peers, social interactions); or (4) your own clear thinking and conscious choices. Of the four, the social constructs of society have by far the greatest influence on most people, while clear thinking and conscious choices have the least.

By "social construct" we mean the dominant worldview held by society that constructs and embeds meaning and form into people's life experiences. A society's social construct determines its structures and processes—its forms of government, education, finance, health care, legal system, religion, customs, and, of course, how its organizations are designed and run. Social constructs determine what is ultimately viewed as good and evil, right or wrong; how people relate to nature; who has certain rights and privileges and who doesn't; how life works; whether there is a God or not and what one must do to be in good favor with him (or her).

Social constructs are not necessarily based on an accurate perception of reality any more than is an individual's worldview. Societies can make erroneous assumptions about reality, just as an individual can. For most people, the dominant social construct of their society permeates and controls nearly every aspect of how they see the world.

There are exceptions, however. The first is when a person's family system or community adheres to different fundamental assumptions than her society does, *and* she has a stronger affinity for her family or community than she does for society at large. In this case, being more closely aligned to her subgroup (her family), she may reject society's worldview and adopt the subgroup's. This phenomenon occurred in grand scale in the 1960s with the hippie movement. Many children who grew up in hippie communities adopted different social constructs than others in their generation who were raised in traditional families and communities.

Another exception occurs in strong-minded, independent thinkers who are exposed to worldviews that are different from their societies. These people, after much conscious, focused deliberation about various alternative views of reality, may adopt a different worldview from their society. Often, such people are seen as rebels or visionaries, such as Martin Luther King, Jr., or Ralph Nader. But even in such strong-willed, independent-minded people, the effects of society's dominant worldview can still linger. For any person, strong-willed or not, unraveling society's influence from their personal *choice* about how they view the world requires a dedicated, ongoing practice of introspection and personal transformation.

For the vast majority of people, socially constructed fundamental assumptions about reality are like water is to fish. Because fish are immersed in water from the moment they are born, they have no way to stand outside it and differentiate it from anything else in their experience. They cannot know water as something separate from them because it is all they have ever known. Even though water is at the center of a fish's way of life, it is invisible to them.

Similarly, people are born into society's fundamental assumptions about reality without ever knowing that these assumptions exist. They are immersed in the pervasive impact of these assumptions from the first breath they take. People grow up, for the most part, never really knowing that they have fundamental assumptions. It could be said that people *accept* society's fundamental assumptions, but that implies that they are *conscious* of them. And for most people, that simply isn't true.

Being conscious of your fundamental assumptions is not important, unless, of course, they do not portray reality accurately or they lead to undesired outcomes. Because your fundamental assumptions frame the world you live in and the meaning you find in it, if they are inaccurate, then you are living in a reality that is a figment of your imagination. This misperception of reality can cause you to respond to circumstances in ways that are not congruent with what is required. This is all too often the case in leading transformational change.

A New Set of Assumptions About Reality

The Industrial Mindset fueled the Industrial Revolution. It was conceived and adopted by society during the time of the Renaissance and Enlightenment and has been modern society's dominant view of reality for the past two and a half centuries.

The Industrial Mindset has delivered tremendous benefit to society. Its greatest achievements have been the massive scientific breakthroughs that have advanced technology and generated incredible material production. The Industrial Mindset, however, has also led to many of the significant disasters and difficulties of modern times, such as pollution and destruction of the eco-system, overpopulation, weapons of mass destruction, and the alienation of people. This mindset has been both a blessing and a curse, which is true of any beneficial breakthrough that is unconsciously used or applied too extensively. Any strength, when overapplied, becomes a weakness.

The Industrial Mindset grew out of a scientific paradigm about the nature of reality that was based on the scientific knowledge of the 17th Century. But science has progressed, and so must society's worldview in order to solve the challenges of the 21st Century. Meg Wheatley says it well:

> "Each of us lives and works in organizations designed from Newtonian images of the universe. We manage by separating things into parts, we believe that influence occurs as a direct result of force exerted from one person to another, we engage in complex planning for a world that we keep expecting to be predictable, and we search continually for better methods of objectively perceiving the world. These assumptions come to us from seventeenth-century physics, from Newtonian mechanics. They are the base from which we design and manage organizations, and from which we do research in all of the social sciences. Intentionally or not, we work from a worldview that has been derived from the natural sciences.
>
> "However, the science has changed. If we are to continue to draw from the sciences to create and manage organizations, to design research, and to formulate hypotheses about organizational design, planning, economics, human nature, and change processes (the list can be much longer), then we need to at least ground our work in the science of our times. We need to stop seeking after the universe of the seventeenth century and begin to explore what has become known to us in the twentieth century. We need to expand our search for the principles of organization to include what is presently known about the universe." (1994, p.6)

The Emerging Mindset is based on the collective research of a number of scientists in different scientific disciplines. A number of exceptional books provide a review of this literature. Two of our favorites are Margaret Wheatley's *Leadership and the New Science* (1994) and Gary Zukav's *Dancing Wu Li Masters* (1979). The copy below lists several of the most notable scientists exploring and writing about the edges of scientific understanding.

Scientists Exploring Leading-Edge Discoveries

Niels Bohr, Werner Heisenberg (1958), and Erwin Schroedinger—pioneers in the field of quantum physics

Ilya Prigogine (Prigogine & Stenger, 1984), 1977 winner of the Nobel prize—self-organizing systems or "dissipative structures"

Biologist Rupert Sheldrake (1995)—exploration of field theory, in particular the articulation of morphogenetic fields

Systems scientist Eric Jantsch (1980)—descriptions of autopoiesis and further work on self-organizing systems

British physicist David Bohm (1980)—study of the implicate order found at the most fundamental level of life

---

Although the Emerging Mindset is substantiated by the leading edge of contemporary science, it also contains essential components of the worldview that existed in pre-modern human history, most notably, mindset. The Industrial Mindset, on the other hand, which initiated the modern era, does not recognize the role and impact of mindset. Before we outline the Industrial and Emerging Mindsets in detail, let's explore this pre-modern worldview to demonstrate how mindset has been neglected in modern times, and how it is now being reinstated by the Emerging Mindset worldview back into its rightful place as an essential component of reality.

The Great Chain of Being

Prior to the Industrial Mindset, humankind possessed an almost consensual worldview across cultures, geographic regions, and time about the fundamental nature of reality. Huston Smith (1992) describes this commonly held worldview of virtually all of the great pre-modern wisdom traditions as the "Great Chain of Being." The Great Chain of Being describes reality as comprised of various levels, beginning with matter, then moving to body, emotions, mind, and spirit.

This is not to say that all pre-modern societies described this Great Chain of Being in the same way; they did not. Some described reality using three levels, others used twelve. The point, however, is that virtually all described reality as comprised of both an external reality (matter and body) as well as an internal reality (mind, heart, spirit).

This acknowledgement and attention to both internal and external reality summarizes our core message about what is needed to lead conscious transformation. Leaders must attend to both aspects of reality. If leaders attend only to external reality, then by definition, their efforts cannot be fully conscious because they are leaving consciousness out of the equation from the beginning. Attending only to external reality denies a major part of the human experience. This does not expand conscious awareness; it reduces it to selective awareness.

As Ken Wilber (1998, p. 9) describes it: "Such has been the dominant worldview, in one variation or another, for most of humankind's history and prehistory. It is the backbone of the 'perennial philosophy,' the nearly universal consensus about reality held by humanity for most of its time on this earth. Until, that is, the rise of modernity in the West."

The Industrial Mindset radically altered this pre-modern worldview. What actually happened during the transition to "modern times," marked by the Renaissance, Enlightenment, and Industrial Revolution? How did society's fundamental assumptions about reality change?

Matter, and the scientific method that dominates the study of matter, became omnipotent. External reality, and the objective measurement of it, became the mainstay of modern thought. The Great Chain of Being collapsed into a single dimension—material form—and the internal world lost its rightful place as a legitimate aspect of reality. As Wilber (1998, p. 10) states, "In its place was a 'flatland' conception of the universe as composed basically of matter (or matter/energy), and this material universe, including material bodies and material brains, could best be studied by science, and science alone. Thus, in the place of the Great Chain reaching from matter to God, there was now matter, period. And so it came to pass that the worldview known as scientific materialism became, in whole or part, the dominant official philosophy of the modern West."

Over the past two hundred or more years, society has invalidated internal reality and has recognized only external reality as important. Society has focused on individual behavior, performance, and results (external), yet has mostly disregarded the impact of people's thoughts, feelings, and beliefs (internal). At the organizational level, society has recognized as critical an organization's market share, profitability, and structure (external), yet has overlooked the impact of its culture, morale, and ethics (internal).

Why is this notion of the collapse of the Great Chain of Being important to leaders and consultants to transformation? Very simply, today's leaders have been born into a socially accepted worldview that does not accurately portray the very nature of reality that they are attempting to transform. Without realizing it, leaders enter the game of leading transformation with a game plan designed for the wrong game. They craft change strategies that are based on erroneous assumptions and misinterpretations of the transformational dynamics they face. Specifically, leaders put their primary focus on the gross, external reality of tasks and activities (content) and neglect the basic internal dynamics of human beings and organizational culture (people). Furthermore, as we shall soon see, the mindset of scientific method and materialism has also caused leaders to overlook the critical process dynamics of change (process).

In our discussions of change strategy in the Introduction, we stated that transformation requires attention to all three components—content, people, and process. We suggest that change leaders cannot neglect any one of these components of a comprehensive change strategy, yet the Industrial Mindset neglects two of them!

Four Cornerstones of the Industrial Mindset

The scientific method, taught to high school students everywhere, is the industrial era's foundation for gathering valid data about the world and the essential tool of scientific research. Webster defines scientific method as the "principles and procedures for the systematic pursuit of knowledge involving the recognition and formulation of a problem, the collection of data through observation and experiment, and the formulation and testing of hypotheses." As a tool, the scientific method has been the mechanism by which thousands of beneficial scientific discoveries have been made. In the 17th Century, when science became king, scientific method became the basis for how knowledge about the external world was acquired.

Over time, the repetitive, habitual, and institutionally required use of the scientific method cemented four cornerstones of the Industrial Mindset into the very fabric of how society views reality, which, of course, subsequently dictates how leaders traditionally view and lead change. We will explore each of these critical aspects of the Industrial Mindset as a precursor to a more detailed discussion of both the Industrial and Emerging Mindsets.

1. *Cornerstone: The internal reality of human consciousness is not valid.* Scientific method relies on observable data, stating that if it is not observable, then it is not valid. Over the decades, this belief has become so engrained in society's thinking that anything not observable has lost its validity. Aspects of personal reality considered to be invalid include feelings, thoughts, desires, values, relationships, fears, motivations, and intuitions. For example, the norms of most organizations have dictated that people leave their personal (internal) lives at home. Aspects of organizational reality that leaders have historically considered unimportant include culture, shared values, politics, ethics, employee buy-in, and morale. Only in the past decade or so have internal, unobservable aspects of human consciousness become valid areas of attention in organizations. These areas have received recent attention because the rapid pace of change has exacerbated these internal dynamics to the point where they have negatively impacted the valid, external aspects of profitability and results.

2. *Cornerstone: Scarcity.* The Industrial Mindset sees the world from the fear-inducing, scarcity perspective that there are not enough resources or solutions to create what is desired. Scientific method focuses on current problems rather than on positive futures. Problem identification, an essential ingredient of the scientific method, has become so engrained in our everyday thinking that it is difficult for people to focus on what *is* working. No matter how good something is, people's minds keep looking for what needs to be fixed or improved. The nightly television news and daily newspapers are pervasive examples of this tendency. Good news just doesn't sell. Bad news does. People hunger to know about the problems of the world and hardly notice their solutions or the good things being created around them.

    Although this compulsion to see what isn't working can, and should, lead to beneficial improvement, there are serious negative side effects when this tendency is overdone. People begin to adopt the worldview that the world is inherently inadequate and insufficient. With this mindset, there is little positive foundation on which people can build positive futures. They become merely *reactive* to the negativities of the world and lose their *creative* capacity to generate compelling possibilities and solutions.[1]

---

[1]The growing practice of "Appreciative Inquiry" was created to counteract this debilitating force. For further information, see Watkins and Mohr (2001).

3. *Cornerstone: Separate Parts.* The Industrial Mindset views reality through the lens of separation, where the pieces are more visible and important than their relationships or the whole of which they are a part. Scientific method gathers data and furthers knowledge by dissecting reality into smaller and smaller pieces and isolating one phenomenon from another to discover how each works. For example, in medicine, researchers and doctors primarily study the individual components of the body (the endocrine system, nervous system, respiratory system, circulatory system, and so forth). They isolate their area of study and become specialists in very narrow disciplines. Few medical doctors or researchers actually study how the various bodily systems work together. The relationship between the parts and the integrated system dynamics of the whole body are neglected in the name of their specialization.

   This protocol of separating external reality into component parts and making the study of the parts the priority has engrained into society a worldview that places the success of the part over the success of the whole. In organizations, this manifests as people fighting for *their* ideas, *their* projects, *their* departments, *their* business units. People often do not consider whether their individual pursuit is what is best for the whole enterprise. Furthermore, this orientation causes leaders to focus on the *boundaries* between things rather than on the *relationships* that connect them. Believing the parts are unrelated, leaders then manage the parts (the functions, processes, lines of business) separately and neglect the interdependencies that contribute so significantly to their individual and collective success. Because the parts are easier to manage than the whole system, this further reinforces leaders' attention to the parts at the expense of the whole system.

4. *Cornerstone: Discrete Events.* The Industrial Mindset causes leaders to perceive change as a series of discrete and isolated events, negating their ability to influence the true process dynamics that govern the achievement of their desired results. Scientific method takes static snapshots of reality and analyzes them for knowledge in isolation from what went before or after in time. Rather than isolating a phenomenon and separating it from others across space, this cornerstone isolates and separates phenomenon across time.

   This is akin to the difference between using still frame photography versus motion pictures to depict reality. The still picture of the single frame does not portray the system dynamics at play. This freeze-frame attribute of scientific method has caused society, and leaders, to lose sight of the fact that life and change are a continuous process, where one event flows seamlessly out of the last and into the next. Thus leaders inadvertently assume that change is a string of discrete events and don't see or attend to the connections between those events over time and rely on singular, isolated interventions (events) to influence change. With this view, leaders cannot effectively work the connections between change events to build momentum toward their goal. They cannot leverage the success of earlier events to set up and add to the success of future events naturally.

Four Cornerstones of the Emerging Mindset

The four cornerstones of the Emerging Mindset clearly tell a different story about reality:

1. *Consciousness Is Causative:* Mindset directly impacts results.

2. *Abundance:* There are more than enough resources and solutions to achieve desired results.

3. *Relationship and Wholeness:* The parts are interconnected and form integrated wholes that are more than the sum of their parts.

4. *Continuous Process:* Everything is in constant motion and specific process dynamics influence how results are produced over time.

These four pillars of the Emerging Mindset are clearly the opposite of those found in the Industrial Mindset. However, the Emerging Mindset does not negate or replace the Industrial Mindset. It simply transcends and includes it. The Emerging Mindset takes the cornerstones of the Industrial Mindset and adds to them. How can this be when the two seem so in conflict with one another? How can reality be both infused with consciousness and void of it, scarce and abundant, separate and whole, a continuous process and a series of discrete events? The answer to this question unleashes tremendous insight and capability for successful change leadership!

The Emerging Mindset acknowledges that certain aspects of reality are governed by the cornerstones of the Industrial Mindset. It isn't that the Industrial Mindset is wrong. It simply has been applied too broadly. A critical breakthrough of the Emerging Mindset is the knowledge of when to apply which mindset. As a leader of transformation, the key is to discern how to use the wisdom of each mindset to build effective change strategy.

The determination of which mindset applies is based on whether one is interfacing with an open system or a closed system. A closed system is isolated from its larger environment and cannot freely exchange energy, information, or matter with it. An open system, however, has a two-way relationship with its environment. Open systems import energy, matter, and information from their environments, continually renewing the system's capacity for change and transformation. Machines are closed systems; living systems are open systems. Human systems are inherently open. However, they are often treated as closed systems by placing rigid, artificial boundaries between them and their environments. Examples of closed human systems include authoritarian government, prisons, religious dogma, production lines with tight operating procedures, and sequestered juries. Clearly the boundaries around these "closed" human systems are not impermeable. New information does leak into authoritarian governments and sequestered juries, which then causes change in those supposed closed systems. Examples of open human systems include continuous improvement teams, community based schools, democratic governments, and businesses using the worldwide web, all of which show an active interchange between the human system and its environment.

The Industrial Mindset accurately portrays the dynamics of closed systems. However, society has mistakenly applied the Industrial Mindset to open systems (living systems). The impact of this mistake on organizations (a human system) was minimal when leaders focused primarily on leading current operations, developmental change, or transitional change. These activities could largely be isolated from the impact of their larger environment. However, with the proliferation of transformational change, driven directly by the volatile marketplace, the drastic over-extension of the Industrial Mindset has become painfully evident.

Leaders cannot lead transformation successfully from a closed system perspective because marketplace dynamics, the ultimate drivers of the change, are so volatile and influential on the current and future success of the organization. There is, and must be, an open-systems relationship between the organization and its marketplace.

The organization needs the information and energy the dynamic marketplace provides for two critical reasons. First, in transformation, the future state is emergent and cannot be predicted because of the dynamic changes occurring within the marketplace. These marketplace shifts provide the wake-up calls that assist the organization to discover its ultimate destination. If the organization were sequestered from the impact of the marketplace, it wouldn't get these wake-up calls and would assume what its best future might be without this vital information.

Second, in transformation, the magnitude of the change required by the marketplace is so significant that people's mindsets (leaders and employees alike) must transform to even see and understand the scope of change required. The information that drives this transformation of mindset comes directly from the dynamic and changing environment. With a closed system orientation, this new information wouldn't enter the organization to catalyze the mindset transformation required.

For these reasons, transformation is only possible from an open systems view. Isolating the organization from its environment when that environment is radically changing or blocking the flow of information inside the organization is a sure path to failure.

Comparing the Two Mindsets

Table 5.1 provides a summary of the key elements of the Industrial and the Emerging Mindsets. The key elements of each mindset function together to create an overall assumption, or mental model, about reality. Although it is important to understand each item, the overall gestalt is most critical.

Table 5.1. Comparison of the Industrial and Emerging Mindsets

The Industrial Mindset "Reality As a Great Machine"	The Emerging Mindset "Reality As a Living System"
Separate Parts	Wholeness/Relationship
Power and Control	Co-Create and Participate
Certainty/Predictability	Uncertainty/Probability
Objective/Knowable	Subjective/Mysterious
Discrete Events	Continuous Process
Entropy	Self-Organization
Order into Chaos	Order out of Chaos
External Causation	Internal Causation
Scarcity	Abundance

Review Table 5.1 before reading the following descriptive paragraphs, remembering that each mindset has a valid application and that the Emerging Mindset actually acknowledges the specific domain (closed systems) where the Industrial Mindset applies. We set the two mindsets in contrast to one another in the diagram not to denote that one replaces the other, but to highlight the critical differences in their core perspectives. There is no priority to the key elements; in fact, the four cornerstones are embedded within the lists. We have placed the key elements in the order that we believe provides the clearest description of each mindset. Where possible, we combine key elements in the descriptions below to promote clarity.

1. Separate Parts vs. Wholeness/Relationship. The Industrial Mindset is based on the core mental model of *"reality as a great machine,"* comprised of *separate parts* that do not necessarily relate to or influence one another. The boundaries between the parts are most prevalent because they separate the different components and thereby provide the greatest sense of control. Bridges between components are few and far between and of lesser importance.

The worldview of the Emerging Mindset is based on the new science's understanding of *"reality as a living system."* Everything is in *relationship,* connected and interdependent. Nothing exists in isolation. *Wholeness* is the essential nature of reality. In disciplines from chemistry (Prigogine) to biology (Sheldrake) to quantum physics (Bohm) to brain research (Pribram) to the Gaia hypothesis (Lovelock), the greatest minds today are demonstrating that life is a unified and interdependent whole. In this mindset, bridges and connections are more prevalent and important than boundaries.

2. Power and Control vs. Co-Create and Participate; 3. Certainty/Predictability vs. Uncertainty/Probability; and 4. Objective/Knowable vs. Subjective/Mysterious. The early advocates of the Industrial Mindset believed that science, by separating and dissecting the phenomena of life, would ultimately discover the basic building blocks of life, solving all of its mysteries and giving them complete *power and control* over it. They believed that science would ultimately deliver the "user's manual" for the "great machine of life" that would enable them to become king of their universe. They believed that if they could fully understand the laws governing the great machine then they could *predict* the machine's behavior, thereby becoming able to cause it to do what they wanted. If phenomena were discovered that did not fit their machine model, the proponents of the Industrial Mindset simply noted that science did not yet know enough about the situation. They believed that all of reality was *objective* and *knowable* and that eventually science would dissect reality into small enough pieces to discover the laws that placed all anomalies in their rightful place in the machinery.

In the contemporary research of quantum physics, scientists have dissected reality beyond what Isaac Newton and other fathers of the Industrial Mindset could have imagined. There are no building blocks of life! Life is a web of interconnected relationships described as a "continuous dance of energy" (Capra, 1983, p. 91). All people are part of this dance; everyone participates in it. Furthermore, reality is subjective and mysterious and matter behaves according to the mindset of the viewer who is observing it (that seamless connection between perception and reality described in Chapter Four). Reality is *uncertain.* It is so dynamic and unpredictable that people can only assume *probabilities* of future events. Predictability is an illusion. Therefore, people cannot gain power over and control of reality. They can only be in relationship to it and, through their relationship, work with reality to facilitate desired outcomes. Instead of being controllers and managers of the great machine, people are *co-creators* with the living system of which they are a part.

5. Discrete Events vs. Continuous Process. In the Industrial Mindset, time is separated and bounded, just as space is. Life is seen as *discrete events*, each with a clearly manageable beginning, middle, and end. Because reality is viewed through static snapshots in time, the influence of past events on current and future circumstances is often overlooked.

In the Emerging Mindset, people see life as "the undivided wholeness in flowing movement" Bohm (1980, p. 11). Life is seen as one *continuous process*, with innumerable subprocesses that are all interconnected and related. Nothing stops; everything is in constant motion. What occurs in one moment naturally progresses into and influences what occurs in the next moment.

6. Entropy vs. Self-Organization. The Industrial Mindset believes that *entropy* is the direction of activity. Sadi Carnot, the French physicist, formulated this second law of thermodynamics in 1824. Put simply, this is the law of "decay over time." As Michael Talbot (1986, p. 133) states: "Closed systems tend toward greater states of disorder—a drop of water in a beaker becomes more dispersed; rooms tend to become messier, not cleaner; and mountains are steadily worn down by the wind and pulverized into sand." This worldview is the seed of pessimism and the notion that life is on a steady treadmill toward greater chaos and despair. Meg Wheatley (1992, p. 76) paraphrases this mindset: "Life goes on, but it's all downhill."

In open systems, the second law of thermodynamics does not apply. Open systems import energy, matter, and information from their environments that continually renew the system's capacity for transformation and new life at a more complex and ordered level. Metaphorically speaking, open systems do not die; they *self-renew* (transform). They use incoming energy and information to evolve and *self-organize* into a higher order that better fits and serves their changing environment.

7. Order into Chaos vs. Chaos out of Order and 8. External Causation vs. Internal Causation. In the Industrial Mindset, life is seen as moving from order into chaos. Because entropy is causing this chaotic world to move toward destruction, people must apply external force to keep the world from falling apart (external causation). People must literally hold the pieces together if they hope to maintain any sense of stability and order, both of which are highly prized. And because only external reality is valid, what people think and feel doesn't matter. They should just do the work expected of them and not voice their concerns or feelings.

Living systems are inherently order-finding; they self-organize from within, naturally making order out of chaos. Stability is not a desire, for growth happens in a living system through disruptions and perturbations of its current reality. The disorder of chaos is the source of renewal; the next order of evolution emerges from the chaos. Furthermore, internal causation governs living systems. Incoming information (open system) is the creative force that transforms them. Because living systems are infused with consciousness, as new information arrives, the consciousness of the organism evolves accordingly, and the new mindset causes new behavior, actions, and results. Ultimately, the new consciousness causes a transformation to occur. So not only is the internal reality valid, but it is the source of all change.

9. Scarcity vs. Abundance. The "universe as machine" worldview is fueled by the belief in *scarcity*, that there is "not enough" to keep the machine operating. Engines do run out of gas; closed systems do consume their resources. The scarcity mindset believes, in the extreme, that the environment is a hostile, dog-eat-dog world where only the fittest survive. Threat is a prime motivator. Organisms must struggle against the forces of entropy and chaos, as well as fight each other for limited resources. This scarcity mentality also applies to people; they are "not enough" either. At the core, people cannot be trusted to succeed. Left to their own devices, people will behave poorly. Therefore, if the leader doesn't exert authority over them, people, too, will manifest the forces of entropy and chaos. It is only by sheer force of power and control and will that leaders get people to do good and perform well.

In contrast, living systems are viewed as *abundant*. They are complete and whole as they are, possessing everything they need to survive and evolve with their changing environment. As the environment changes, the system will import what it needs and transform to continue to thrive. Plenty of resources exist, and by removing any artificial boundaries between the system and its environment, a system can diffuse its tendency to decay and import the required energy and information for renewal. Resources can be found, and it is up to the system to use them creatively to survive and thrive. In addition, people are seen as capable, inherently good, possessing the ability to learn what they need to know, and adaptable to change. They are creative, competent, and committed to building a positive future. Provide people with adequate information and support, and they will self-organize to produce whatever is necessary to adapt to their changing environment.

The Ten Principles of Conscious Transformation

Viewing people, organizations, and change through the lens of the Emerging Mindset increases leaders' conscious awareness of transformational dynamics. It promotes change leadership behavior and change strategies that are congruent with what transformation requires, which both increases the probability of success and the avoidance of mistakes.

After being raised in cultures governed by the Industrial Mindset, how do change leaders adopt the Emerging Mindset? One effective way is to use operating principles or ground rules based on the Emerging Mindset to design and facilitate their transformational change efforts. In our twenty years of experience coaching change leaders and consulting to their transformation efforts, we have identified ten such operating principles. Inevitably, when we see transformational change efforts working, we can trace the success to these principles. When the process is sputtering, the cause is more often than not because the change leaders have made decisions or taken action inconsistent with these principles.

These principles are not the answer to *all* troubles in transformation. Transformational processes are just too complex for such a simple solution. However, our experience demonstrates that adhering to these principles increases the probability that the design of a transformation process and its rollout will go as well as can be expected.

These operating principles are like decision criteria or design requirements for the transformation process. In fact, we believe that all of your decisions and actions as a transformational change leader should be governed by these principles. By integrating these operating principles into how you design and implement change, you will unleash the positive influence of the Emerging Mindset into your organization's transformation.

1. Wholeness

- Promote what is best for the whole system;
- See the system and its components as one integrated entity;
- Treat individual components of the system as wholes themselves; and
- Design one integrated overall change.

Implications for Change Leaders: Even though the overall transformation process likely includes numerous individual change initiatives, each initiative must clearly support the enterprise's primary transformation objective. Employees must overtly experience that all change initiatives and activities fit into and support the whole system's transformation, be it the whole enterprise, a line of business, or a region. Everything must be linked to the overall objective of the system being transformed. If any activity does not link, then change leaders must modify, stop, or replace that activity with ones that do support the whole.

2. Interconnectedness

- Integrate and coordinate individual initiatives and activities; integrate organizational/technical initiatives with cultural/human initiatives, enterprise-wide initiatives with area-specific initiatives, corporate center initiatives with line or business unit initiatives;
- Think about impacts across boundaries; see everything as connected; consider the distant impacts of local actions, and vice versa; and
- Build and sustain relationships between organizational entities to enhance mutual and system-wide effectiveness.

Implications for Change Leaders: Change leaders must fully attend to the interdependencies of change processes. Change leaders must build bridges across functions, processes, stakeholder groups, and change initiatives to ensure collaboration, information sharing, and shared accountability for enterprise outcomes. In addition, change leaders must be sure to establish the infrastructure and governance systems to accomplish this integration of mutually dependent components.

3. Multi-Dimensional

- Attend to all the internal and external realities (physical, emotional, mental, and spiritual) at the levels of the individual, relationship, team, whole system, and marketplace/environment.

Implications for Change Leaders: Change leaders must expand their focus and competency to be able to attend to not only external reality (content, structure, technology), but to the internal realities of individual mindset, interpersonal dynamics, and team and organizational culture. They must discern the systems dynamics of their organization at all levels, as well as the influence of their marketplace and environment. Furthermore, change leaders must see the potential impacts between the larger and smaller systems within their organization. Cognizant of these forces, they must design and implement a transformational change strategy that attends to the needs of each dimension in an integrated way.

4. Continuous Process Through Time

- Think about impacts across time; think ahead and think behind; understand the influence of the past on the current situation and the impact of current decisions or actions on the future;

- Build momentum and critical mass; leverage interactions between people and events to create a positive "snowball" effect over time; plan events so that each adds to the success of the next;

- Go slow to go fast; take the time to build the upstream foundations for downstream success; pace activities according to the organization's true capacity to succeed;

- Build off the best of the past and present; and

- Honor the natural order of death and rebirth in change; support the process to proceed by supporting what needs to die and what needs to grow.

Implications for Change Leaders: Change leaders must minimize their attempts to influence transformation with isolated events. For example, when change leaders decide to communicate about their change effort, they must first evaluate previous communications for how the content and style of delivery were received by the audience and then tailor the process and content of their current communications accordingly. Furthermore, they must plan their future communications to reinforce the message over time and create further buy-in. In short, they must think of communications as a continuous process. The same is true of all transformational activities.

Transformation is often accompanied by a sense of urgency. Unchecked, this time pressure usually slows the process. Change leaders must learn when to "go slow to go fast." Often, taking the necessary time upstream to establish the proper conditions for success pays off handsomely downstream.

One such upstream condition is celebrating the past. Change often carries a tone that the past was somehow insufficient (why else would we be changing?). Change leaders must overtly celebrate the positive attributes of the past and present so that people can build off their accomplishments as they move into the future. The death of the old must be reframed in the minds of employees from something bad to the necessary positive birth of something better and more aligned with current and future needs.

5. Continuously Learn and Course Correct

- Proactively generate useful information and feedback and share it across boundaries to promote learning; remove barriers to sharing information;

- Always seek the value in mistakes and failures; befriend and explore aberrant information as guidance for future success; and

- Pilot possibilities; float test balloons; support forays into new ways of designing or operating the new state.

Implications for Change Leaders: Thinking that reality can ultimately be known causes change leaders to fall into the trap of thinking that their current content, people, and process answers are fixed and complete. They forget that all answers are only temporary best guesses, because new information will likely come along and alter or improve the answers they currently hold.

Instead of putting such importance on being right, change leaders must focus on learning. They must build learning communities around key transformation issues and create structures and processes to share insights and build best practices across boundaries. Mistakes or difficulties must be explored, their causes discovered, and better approaches designed from the information they generate. People must be encouraged to take risks and attempt new practices in all twenty-one dimensions, even though they are likely to make mistakes as they learn. Plus, the results of their forays, positive or negative, can be made available for everyone's insight.

Because information generation and sharing are integral to learning, change leaders need to build information generation processes that feed directly into their process design and facilitation practices. There are numerous ways to promote learning through information exchange. Examples include:

- Give employees direct access to the marketplace by sending them on benchmarking missions, putting them on teams to study industry trends or exposing them to competitors' strategies;

- Employ open book management, exposing employees to your business strategies, reasons for them, and the business model they employ, as well as the financial performance of the organization;

- Create an enterprise-wide project integration infrastructure so individual change initiatives continually share status reports and other information and resources with one another; and

- Deliver continuous "mid-process" communications about the marketplace and the change effort, rather than only share information when an answer or solution has been formalized.

6. Abundance

- Think abundantly; whatever is needed exists somewhere in the system or its environment; seek it out and find it; and

- Assume there are enough resources, time, energy, and opportunity until you discover otherwise; then get more creative and go find what you think is lacking.

Implications for Change Leaders: Change leaders must trust in the future. They must operate from the mindset that no matter how difficult or challenging their circumstances, they believe in "abundance." They perceive their circumstances through the lens of their being "enough," expecting that there is a solution available and that, with support, the people in the organization will discover and implement that solution. Change leaders must trust people, provide them with resources, and grant them the authority to use those resources appropriately. Leaders who hold this abundant mindset and model it through their behavior will consistently create the fundamental internal mental and cultural conditions for successful transformation. They will unleash the full potential of the organization to discover and optimally use its resources and talent.

7. Balance Planning with Attending to Emerging Dynamics

- Plan ahead, but be observant and respond in the moment; alter the desired state and change strategy as new information emerges;

- Exert appropriate influence; determine whether you need to "make the change happen, help it happen, or let it happen" (Beckhard & Harris, 1987); and

- Embrace dynamics that seem to be in conflict, such as organizational/human pressures, short-term/long-term needs or goals, speed/thoroughness; let each polarity be heard rather than champion one extreme; allow the tension between polarities to resolve and move the transformation forward.

Implications for Change Leaders: Change leaders must stop assuming that they can control transformation. Project thinking causes change leaders to assume that they can design a change plan, then implement it with minimal variation. In transformation, the environment is so dynamic that continually learning about and course correcting the plan is fundamental. Leaders cannot be certain about what will transpire in their marketplace, nor can they predict how people will react to their various change interventions. Therefore, they cannot know in advance exactly what will be required as their transformation unfolds.

Change plans must be expected to shift, and the learning must alter those plans. Furthermore, change leaders must design practices that support real-time course corrections throughout implementation. This will build their organization's capacity to respond to whatever occurs.

In order to balance planning with real-time course correcting, change leaders must ensure that their transformation efforts behave as open systems, where there is an open exchange of information and ideas between people and their environment. This information exchange will naturally influence people's thinking and decisions, causing the organization to evolve appropriately. This requires that change leaders remove barriers to information and energy exchange, as well as remove control mechanisms that stifle the natural growth of their organization to its next higher order.

Change leaders must allow, support, and even encourage chaos as it emerges, rather than attempt to control and stifle the messes that are inherent in transformation. Change leaders must encourage chaos and listen to its message so it can shake up the organization as the transformation requires. This disruption, when allowed to express itself and be heard, is the source of the needed wake-up calls that provide the organization the insight, learning, and course corrections it needs. Change leaders who understand this dynamic maximize people's exposure to dissonant information because they realize that seeding this information in a critical mass of people's minds is the catalyst of significant and sustainable change. Change leaders must befriend chaos, for out of chaos the Phoenix inevitably rises.

Such chaos often results from conflicting or competing interests. Change leaders must encourage the people representing these interests to share an open dialogue, not from a positional stance of trying to win the argument, but from the "service to the whole" perspective of openly sharing how their views would add value to the overall transformation. By letting the conflicting positions be fully heard and by encouraging people to focus on the overall transformation's success, the right solution can occur unimpeded.

8. Lead as if the Future Is Now

- Ensure that your change strategy models and promotes the desired culture;
- Design your change process to demonstrate to the organization that the desired culture already exists;
- Model the desired state; walk the talk of the change; and
- Write your vision statement and stretch goals in the present tense.

Implications for Change Leaders: Many change leaders aspire to create a new culture and communicate this to employees, then manage their transformation based on the old culture's norms. This demonstrates to the organization that nothing has really changed. A classic example is when leaders say they want a culture of participation and inclusion, then design their transformation process with little input or involvement outside of the executive ranks. Another common example occurs when change leaders announce that they want to "empower" their employees, yet allow little local control over the design of the future state or how it will be implemented.

Change leaders must model the new culture as they change the old one. They must design and implement the transformation process based on the desired culture's norms, even when this causes conflict with current norms or protocol. They must behave in new-culture ways to demonstrate and reinforce the validity of and their commitment to the new directions.

9. Optimize Human Dynamics

- Account for human dynamics and reactions; plan for human transitions (letting go of the past, rites of passage); create meaning that motivates and inspires people; celebrate successes; assess readiness;

- Maximize participation and ownership throughout the change process; embrace differences; celebrate diversity in all its forms; involve resistors;

- Build and sustain relationships among people, especially across levels and organizational boundaries; allocate time for human connection and needs; and

- Maximize "truth telling," openness, and multi-directional communication; support all parties in speaking openly; resolve conflicts; bring long-standing "undiscussables" into the open and clear them up.

Implications for Change Leaders: Change leaders must incorporate strategies and actions that support human needs throughout the transformation. The transformation process must generate optimal participation and build collective ownership for the change. Leaders must employ foundational OD practices such as attending to relationships, role negotiation, and team building to establish strong working bonds between people across the project community. They must create ritual and rites of passage to honor and let go of the past, allowing for the natural emotional transitions that accompany change. They must build diverse teams and adopt truth-telling practices and open communications across constituent groups. Change leaders can free up enormous amounts of energy in people by bringing historic or current issues out into the open that have previously been off-limits to discussion. This not only clears up any related conflict or confusion, but makes way for new, healthier, and more effective ways of operating.

10. Evolve Mindset

- Legitimize the requirement to address mindset and its impact openly;
- Generate, share, and use relevant information to transform mindset;

- Promote "clear mindedness" in yourself and others; seek clarity between your perception of reality and what is actually occurring;

- Explore assumptions; transform self-limiting beliefs that lead to dysfunctional behavioral patterns and operating practices; and

- Provide personal transformation opportunities to leaders and employees alike; support the evolution of mindset over time.

Implications for Change Leaders: Change leaders must provide significant, ongoing, personal transformation opportunities for themselves and for the people in their organizations. Individual development plans must be fully integrated into the design of the overall transformation. Change leaders must make internal reality overt, accepted, and communicated, like all other valid aspects of organizational life. They must openly discuss their own assumptions and feelings about their marketplace and organization. They must make overt the old cultural dynamics, support people as they discuss what has contributed to these obsolete ways, and clarify how these norms must change. In short, change leaders' foremost responsibility is to make all internal and external dynamics conscious and overt.

Applying These Principles

These ten operating principles provide the foundation for any transformational change methodology. In fact, we believe that any model for guiding conscious transformation will only be effective to the degree that it puts these operating principles into action. Change leadership behavior should reflect these principles as well.

Exhibit 5.1 offers an opportunity for you to reflect on each principle and determine how it might influence your change leadership. Think of a critical aspect of a current or recent transformation process you have led or consulted to; for each principle, consider how it might influence your change strategy. Refer back to the sections above on "Implications for Change Leaders" under each principle. This will trigger your thinking about how you might apply the principles to get the results you desire. Be sure to consider content, people, and process issues and to consider how the principles may impact each. Only attend to the principles that are pertinent to your situation.

Exhibit 5.1. Applying the Operating Principles for Conscious Transformation

The Situation:	The Desired Outcome:

Strategy Planning	
Principle	*Application*
1. Wholeness:	
2. Interconnectedness:	
3. Multi-Dimensional:	
4. Continuous Process:	
5. Learning and Course Correcting:	
6. Abundance:	
7. Planning/Emerging Dynamics:	
8. Lead as if the Future Is Now:	
9. Optimize Human Dynamics:	
10. Evolve Mindset:	

Summary

The fundamental assumptions about reality as articulated by the Industrial Mindset are the basic foundation of most change leaders' mindsets. These assumptions negate change leaders' ability to lead successful transformation because they do not allow change leaders to perceive the accurate dynamics and requirements of transformation. Consequently, change leaders often create change strategies that cannot possibly work in the actual transformational reality they face.

A change leadership breakthrough is needed. Change leaders must become more conscious of their mindsets to acknowledge where the Industrial Mindset has been influencing their worldviews. They must engage in their own personal transformations to overcome the limitations of the Industrial Mindset and integrate the fundamental assumptions of the Emerging Mindset into how they lead people, organizations, and change. In order to support this transformation, change leaders can use the operating principles of conscious transformation described here to guide their decision making and action planning. From this new vantage point, change leaders will be freer to apply either the Industrial Mindset or the Emerging Mindset to their change efforts, as circumstances dictate.

When change leaders begin to view people, organizations, and transformation through the Emerging Mindset, they will more easily develop the essential change leadership skills of process thinking, design, and facilitation. In the next chapter, we will describe these competencies and demonstrate how they are the keystones to facilitating successful transformation.

Section Three
A Process Orientation for Leading Transformation

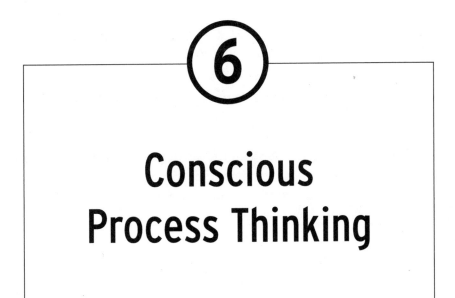

Conscious Process Thinking

AS WE HAVE SAID, CHANGE LEADERS MUST become more conscious of the dynamics of transformation in order to lead it successfully. Leaders must attend to the three critical components of change strategy: *content*, *people*, and *process*. We assume that most leaders are already comfortable and largely competent at addressing the content issues. Consequently, we have focused our discussion on people and process. In Section Two, we attended mostly to mindset, the essence of people dynamics, to discover its critical role in transformation. In this section, we explore process dynamics.

The term "process" has many meanings in organizations. We have deliberated about using the term because it means different things to different people. However, we keep returning to the word because it most precisely describes what we mean when we refer to *conscious process thinking*, the subject of this chapter.

We will begin this chapter by differentiating our use of the term from other uses. Then, we introduce "conscious process thinking" and contrast it with the more common "project thinking." We will describe its similarities to and differences from the more recent breakthrough to "systems thinking," and we will also discuss the tools that each of these thinking orientations use as they relate to change leadership. On this foundation, we will introduce three different change leadership styles to demonstrate how leaders with different styles design and implement transformational change processes differently. We conclude by describing why we believe that a facilitative change leadership style is optimal for most of today's change leaders.

These discussions will set the stage for the next chapter, where we discuss change process models in general and introduce the specific change process model that we have refined over the past two decades, the nine-phase *Change Process Model for Leading Conscious Transformation.*

Differentiating Among Uses of the Word "Process"

The term "process" has many different meanings in the field of organization development and current management theory. For example, reengineering, quality improvement, and team development have different uses of the term. We need to differentiate these various meanings to ensure that we convey our specific meaning clearly, without confusing you. Below is our view of the *other* uses. We encourage you to note your particular meaning(s) of the word "process" from those listed below.

Group Process. The team-building description of how groups of people operate together, relate to one another, and interact (the group's "way of being").

Process Consultation and Observation. The organization development practice of "objectively" observing what goes on when groups of people work together, then devising positive ways to influence their interactions, effectiveness, and relationships.

Process Facilitation. The OD term for leading a pre-designed experience or meeting agenda with the intent of achieving a desired outcome; observing and guiding the dynamics that occur during the rollout of the plan and course correcting to enable the outcome to emerge; leading without controlling.

Process Improvement. The quality movement's practice of defining the action steps required to achieve an end and then refining those steps to achieve the outcome more effectively and efficiently.

Business Process or End-to-End Process. "Macro" processes of the business that cross functional boundaries and outline everything that needs to occur to produce a unified result; such processes are usually the result of "reengineering" the core processes of the organization. Examples include supply chain, customer service, and resource allocation processes.

Processing Information. The thinking and discussing a person or group does to understand, reflect on, make meaning of, or learn about something that has happened or that is needed from them. The information being processed may be about internal or external realities. Examples include debriefing an event, an interaction, or one's emotions.

Personal Process. What an individual goes through as he or she grows emotionally or spiritually, becomes more aware, and learns from life's experiences; self-reflection; consciously learning from and course correcting one's life experiences, mindset, and behavior; self-mastery.

Clearly, the term *process* takes on many meanings in organizations. That, in itself, is a demonstration of the process nature of organizations. You may currently define process in one or more of the ways above. That is fine; all are useful distinctions. However, to receive the full benefit of our next discussion, you may need to put aside, at least temporarily, these or other definitions of process.

Our Definition of Process

Webster offers two relevant definitions of process: (1) "progress, advance; something going on; proceeding"; and (2) "a natural phenomenon marked by gradual changes that lead toward a particular result; a series of actions or operations conducing to an end." The first definition is purely action-oriented, while in the second, action leads to a result.

Webster's results-oriented definition is like our definition of process, which is: *"The natural or intentional unfolding of continuous events toward a desired outcome."* Given the insights of the Emerging Mindset, we understand that open systems continually self-organize to higher levels of order. Through the insights of the Industrial Mindset, we know that closed systems decay. Either way, process has a direction. Or, as Arthur Young (1976) would say, process has purpose.

While process is purposeful action toward a result, the Emerging Mindset suggests that these results are temporary and unstable. Once results are achieved, process moves on to the next result, then the next and the next. This is the nature of process. It continually unfolds. The Emerging Mindset makes it clear that all of life is multi-dimensional process in perpetual motion, an endless weave of processes intermingling with other processes, "the continuous dance of energy" (Capra, 1983, p. 91).

In this process orientation, change is the *norm*. All results, structures, events, and forms are simply snapshots of a continually evolving process. Their appearance of being fixed is an illusion, just a "freeze frame" of a moment in time. Take your organization's structure, for example. Today it may seem fixed and firmly established. Yet last year it was likely different, and next year it will likely change again. If you widen your timeframe, the underlying evolving nature of your organization's structure becomes apparent. Over time, it continually changes between centralization and decentralization, local and global focus, business lines and functional services, standardization and autonomy, all the while evolving (one hopes) to a higher order ability to serve the needs of your changing marketplace and customers. As commonly stated, the only constant in organizations (and life) is change itself. Even "fixed" structures are in dynamic flux.

The Different Levels of Process

There may be a significant time delay between one "physical" change in organizational structure and the next. At first glance, it may seem that the changes occur in surges or jumps, starting and completing, starting and completing. It looks this way if we attend only to the physical domain at the organizational level. But the physical organizational dimension is only one of many. Recall from Chapter Three that there are twenty-one dimensions of activity on which conscious change leaders must focus. On deeper examination, we see that the change in an organization's structure is actually continuous. It is just occurring in different dimensions.

For example, the marketplace is continually providing information that causes people within the organization to question the efficacy of the structure. This promotes dialogue among teams of people, sometimes heated and sometimes harmonious. New ideas are generated by individuals. Studies are done. Conclusions are made. And finally, the organization's structure is changed once again. The process of the organization's physical structure is continually unfolding in various dimensions of reality, building momentum, until finally, on the physical level, the change of structure manifests in a spurt. This continuous nature of process is one of the ten operating principles of conscious transformation that change leaders must understand.

Process is continually unfolding at all levels of the organization's reality—in all twenty-one dimensions. Process is occurring within the *organization* itself, within the *teams and work groups* that exist in the organization, within the multitude of *relationships and interactions* that occur between people, within the *individuals*, as well as within the organization's *environment or marketplace*. On all of these "levels" of the organization's reality, process is occurring within all four of the domains of their existence—within their physical structures, emotional states, assumptions and beliefs, and levels of meaning.

Reactive leaders, viewing organizational behavior through the eyes of the Industrial Mindset, only see the physical changes. Consequently, they usually attend only to the external domain. Conscious leaders, on the other hand, are aware of all the "behind the scenes" (internal) processes that contribute to the overtly manifested external changes.

Our view of "process" includes this multi-dimensional aspect. Therefore, we further expand our definition of process: "The natural or intentional unfolding of continuous events, *within all dimensions of reality,* toward a desired outcome." Taking a "process orientation," as we mean it, assumes change leaders attune to the process dynamics of each of the twenty-one domains as they are relevant to their transformation.

When change leaders are conscious of the multi-dimensional aspects of process, they are able to "see" the interdependent process dynamics at play—how the occurrences in one dimension impact the other dimensions. For example, they become sensitive to how a change to the organization's structure impacts employee morale or how altering a team's mission impacts the individual member's level of commitment and satisfaction. With this sensitivity to interdependent process dynamics, change leaders begin to experience that, even though there are many different subprocesses to attend to, all twenty-one collectively comprise one overarching transformational process they must lead. Equipped with this awareness, change leaders have a much greater probability of success because they will be able to see which dimensions must be engaged to move their transformational process forward toward their desired outcomes. The leverage points for change begin to stand out.

► CASE ɪɴ POINT

In one manufacturing organization, the CEO was struggling with how to get the union to commit to the organization's transformation and become full players in it. The union's attitude was, "Our people will simply go get jobs in another company. You may go belly up, but our skills are in high demand throughout this industry." To further exacerbate the problem, a few years previously, the CEO and the union president had a very volatile and openly heated conflict. They had never laid the strike days to rest, and each carried personal grudges against the other.

The company needed a partnership with the union to sustain its success level. And the union, despite the union president's attitude, needed the company as well. Most of its members were long-term company employees and had little other work experience.

The company employed a multi-dimensional process intervention. As you read the following list, notice how processes at various levels of organization and within different domains were employed:

- Breakthrough training was provided for the executive team *and* for the union leaders, which introduced both sides to how their assumptions about each other influenced what they saw about the other and cleared up significant emotional baggage.

- The executive team and union leaders were taught dialogue and communication skills, using their live issues as the topics of conversation.

- The union leaders were invited to the company's visioning conference and had an equal opportunity to influence the content and the emotional wording of the company's purpose and vision.

- A mid-manager who had a longstanding positive relationship with the union president became chair of a union-management partnership team; the CEO did not participate to avoid conflict with the union president, who was a member.

- Coaching support was offered to the union leaders and the executives about their mindsets, emotions, and behavior to help them understand the impact of their styles on the union-management partnership.

- The union's contract negotiations were begun a year in advance to ensure adequate bridge-building and to avoid a last-minute war.

- Union representatives partnered with company supervisors to conduct benchmark studies of best-in-class companies, giving both a shared purpose.

- Plant managers invited their plant stewards to join the plant's change leadership team and influence the future of the plant.

After eighteen months of building momentum in many different dimensions, the physical "surge" occurred and the desired partnership was clearly established. However, at almost any time during that year and a half, there "seemed" to be little tangible progress in the union-management relationship, even though individuals were being impacted. Then, all at once, it occurred for the whole union and all of management.

Taking a multi-dimensional process view, the change leaders were able to turn their small wins in the various dimensions into a very significant and measurable achievement, creating the critical mass required for this transformation. Had they taken a more traditional view, the "lack of progress" would have caused them to "pull the plug" on every one of their individual, discrete attempts to influence the union-management relationship. Seeing multi-dimensional process in action, over time, gave them the wisdom and fortitude to continue until their desired result was achieved. ◄

Three Thinking Orientations

Most change leaders, having "grown up" in mechanistic organizations, take an "event" or project thinking orientation to change rather than a process thinking orientation. Project thinking is most prevalently used by leaders who take a reactive approach to transformation. This inadvertently sets such leaders up to struggle with their transformation from the beginning. Their mindset and, more specifically, their fundamental assumptions about reality (the Industrial Mindset) blind them to the essential process nature of people, organizations, and change, which causes them to apply developmental or transitional change strategies that are insufficient for transformation. In basic terms, they can never build enough momentum to produce the "surge" of change they are seeking.

Over the past two decades, systems thinking emerged and has begun to augment leaders' project thinking orientation. This shift denotes a very significant breakthrough. Systems thinking has vastly expanded leaders' understanding of how organizational systems function as interdependent processes. Yet, from our own process point of view, systems thinking does not deliver the full package of what is needed to lead transformation; by itself, systems thinking often does not produce the recognizable change. An additional orientation that we call *conscious process thinking* is required. Let us explain by first defining project thinking, then systems thinking, and finally conscious process thinking.

Project Thinking

Project thinking is the mode of leadership thinking catalyzed by the Industrial Mindset. It has dominated organizations over the past one hundred years. As much as project thinking has its limitations, it makes its greatest contribution to enhancing operational excellence. Project thinking has structured and organized the activities that have led to many of the significant increases in the production and productivity of the past century. As we describe project thinking as it pertains to leading change, you will notice the familiar attributes of the Industrial Mindset put into action.

Project thinking is linear and sequential. One step follows the other. Time is bounded, marked by separate and discrete change events that are not necessarily impacted by how well activities went before them or of consequence to the design of activities that follow. Detailed change plans are created, complete with roles, tasks, and mandated timelines. Change efforts are managed and controlled to adhere to these plans. Pre-conceived, predictable outcomes are expected. Variation is not tolerated, nor is deviation from the change plan. External force and control are used to prevent otherwise chaotic processes from falling apart. In project thinking, people are often viewed as cogs in the machinery; project thinking neither asks nor encourages people to think outside the boundaries and constraints of their roles in the change plan. A project thinker's intent is to make the change effort "behave" as the leaders require.

Project thinkers run most of today's organizations. In the quest to enhance short-term tangible results, competent project thinkers have *historically* stood out as the superstars. In the more stable environment of the past, they made things happen and, therefore, received the most frequent promotions, even though their people skills might have been lacking. Historically, an organization's succession plan has likely been filled with its organization's best project thinkers.

As today's leaders have had to expand their job responsibilities from improving operations (developmental change) to managing transitional change to leading transformational change, they have naturally applied their project thinking tendencies to the job. Unfortunately, project thinking does not work for leading transformation. In the future, succession plans will not be dominated by the best project thinkers unless they possess systems thinking and process thinking skills as well. Project managers, who have traditionally been project thinkers, can and must expand their repertoire to include systems and process thinking orientations.

Systems Thinking

In the 1960s, Jay Forrester, at the Massachusetts Institute of Technology, broke away from this linear, sequential mode of project thinking and developed "systems dynamics" as a way of mapping the interconnected relationships between components of any system. Forrester (1961) developed the notion of reinforcing and balancing feedback loops to show the dynamic relationship between the parts of a system and how those relationships would impact the overall system through time.

Forrester's development of systems dynamics is indicative of the Emerging Mindset, especially as it relates to the principles of wholeness, connectedness, and continuous process over time. However, even though Forrester spoke often to his students about the importance of their "quality of thinking" as a determinant in their evaluation of a system's dynamics, he did not overtly include mindset or internal reality in his diagnosis of systems. His was primarily an engineering view; he focused mostly on inanimate systems (external reality).

Peter Senge (1990), once a student of Forrester's at M.I.T., popularized the concepts of Forrester's systems dynamics by introducing "systems thinking" to organizational leaders through his book, *The Fifth Discipline*. A significant contribution of Senge's is his inclusion of mental models (mindset) as a valid and essential component of the diagnostic of any human system. Senge included the internal state of people and culture when mapping the forces at play within a system that influence an organization's current reality and the possible achievement of its vision.

Senge's approach to systems thinking is perhaps the most complete available, as it attends to (1) wholeness and interconnectedness across space; (2) continuous process through time; and (3) internal reality. All three variables are equally essential; none can be ignored. However, Senge's is only one of many approaches available today, as systems thinking is now taught by many different people in academic institutions, training companies, and consulting firms.

The variation in what is meant by systems thinking and in how it is taught is huge, depending on whether proponents are focusing on all three variables or just on one or two. All teachers focus on the first, interdependencies of external variables; fewer add the effects of the system's dynamic relationships over time; and fewer still include internal dynamics. Consequently, when most leaders refer to systems thinking, they ponder only interdependencies between external variables and neglect the notions of continuous process and the validity of internal reality. From our point of view, this is an inadequate interpretation of systems thinking.

In our client organizations, we are seeing an evolution of understanding about system dynamics occurring in leaders. Although most leaders still adhere to a project thinking orientation, many are beginning to see the interdependencies across their organizations. And each year there seems to be an increase in leaders' understanding of process and mindset. Consequently we believe that there is a significant evolution—from linear thinking, to seeing interdependencies, to understanding process dynamics over time, to understanding the role and impact of human consciousness—underway in business and industry. The next step in this evolution of change leadership skill will be first about process and then evolve further to include competent attention to mindset.

This evolution is already underway. Clearly, quality, process improvement, and reengineering have all contributed significantly in recent years to leaders' understanding of process.[1] These approaches, however, being the early applications of a process orientation, have been incomplete in three primary ways. First, they have most often been implemented through a linear, cause-and-effect approach applied to one *isolated* process. Although it is valid in some cases (for example, the improvement of one discrete process), it is insufficient to drive transformation. Most often, many interdependencies exist across business processes and other organizational components and a wider systems lens is required for transformation. The tunnel view of isolated process improvement or reengineering is inadequate. So even though leaders speak the language of "end-to-end business processes" and have become proficient in mapping and improving them, they have not adequately learned to see the interdependencies across processes or how to change them concurrently. This limitation, of course, is a product of the influence of project thinking on leaders' emerging understanding of process.

---

[1]The field of OD, although clearly carrying an essential process message, has not had mass acceptance nor impact like these more traditional leadership activities.

Second, these applications of business process improvement methodologies have focused mostly on processes at the systems level, somewhat on processes at the work-group level, and mostly neglected processes at the relationship and individual levels. In other words, they have not attended to all levels. Third, the process methodologies of the past decade have addressed external dynamics, while internal processes at all levels, from cultural to personal, have been mostly overlooked. More complete attention to all twenty-one dimensions of process and their interdependencies and dynamic relationships over time is required.

Conscious Process Thinking

The term "process thinking" has been used in organization development, business process improvement, cognitive theory, and other schools of thought over the past couple of decades. Each of these practices, while extremely valuable in its own right, has focused on only a few of the twenty-one dimensions. We believe that change leaders must be aware of the process dynamics of all dimensions. Therefore, the process thinking required by change leaders is actually "*conscious* process thinking." The word "conscious" denotes being aware of all aspects of process, internal and external, across the levels of individuals, relationships, teams, the whole systems, marketplace, and environment.

Conscious process thinking, then, means "seeing reality as multi-dimensional process, part/wholes connected across space, continuously unfolding through time, affecting both internal and external dimensions at all levels of organizations, from individual to the environment." Wow! What a mouthful. "Flow of the whole across time" is a bit more concise. Or you can think of conscious process thinking as the thinking orientation of the Emerging Mindset, reflecting the ten operating principles of conscious transformation.

We believe that this definition of conscious process thinking is what is intended by the teachers who present the complete three-pronged view of systems thinking outlined earlier. However, we use our term, "conscious process thinking," because it reinforces what we see are the next two critical steps in the evolution of change leadership skill—attention to consciousness and to process.

To summarize, successful change leaders need to view organizations, people, and transformation from this process perspective. They must see their organizations as multi-dimensional, interconnected, conscious "living systems" in constant and perpetual motion. Although they may perceive that external change occurs in surges, they must attend to the often subtle, always continuous processes that drive those surges. This will enable change leaders to build momentum by creating appropriate plans for transformation that guide the "flow" of the change process, internally and externally, at all levels, to their desired outcomes.

Project thinking, systems thinking, and conscious process thinking all have their uses. The following copy lists valuable change leadership applications of each.

Applications of Project Thinking, Systems Thinking, and Conscious Process Thinking

PROJECT THINKING

- Project managing developmental or transitional change according to a timeline and budget, especially when the project can be sequestered from outside influence;

- Assessing resource and time requirements for developmental and transitional change efforts;

- Determining quantifiable and observable measurements; and

- Mapping sequential and parallel change activities.

SYSTEMS THINKING

- Identifying the underlying structure that "causes" an organization's behavior;

- Assessing the interconnected and interdependent relationships within a system and its environment when planning for change or assessing change impacts;

- Assessing leverage points and blockages for change within a system and its environment;

- Identifying key relationships within a system where energy and information currently flow, or must flow in the future, and in what critical directions;

- Identifying possible breakdowns and breakthroughs within a system undergoing change; and

- Identifying cyclical patterns that may help or hinder the performance of a system as it changes.

CONSCIOUS PROCESS THINKING

- Seeing the flow of actions within all twenty-one dimensions that will build momentum toward a result over time;

- Designing conscious transformational change strategy that integrates content, people, and process across all twenty-one dimensions;

- Incorporating the mindset and cultural dimensions of transformation into change strategy;

- Assessing and implementing course corrections to the transformation process as it unfolds;

- Designing strategy for building an organization's capacity for change while it undergoes its current change, especially raising the level of conscious awareness about the breadth and depth of what is required to succeed; and

- Engaging in conscious process design and conscious process facilitation.

Tools of the Thinking Orientations

Each thinking orientation has its own set of tools, all of which can be valuable in transformation when used in the correct applications. They are described below.

Project Management Methodologies

The tool of project thinking is a *project management methodology.* These are extremely effective at organizing discrete actions to achieve a tangible, specific goal on a specific timeline. Project management methodologies provide structured checklists and linear action plans outlining the sequence of what needs to be done. "On time, on budget" is the motto of project management. Project management methodologies require stable, "closed system" settings in which the project can be protected from impacts of changes in its environment. Although dynamic transformational change efforts *can* use project management in isolated applications, traditional project management is not very applicable to the open systems environment of transformation. Project management methodologies are simply too linear and inflexible to drive transformational change.

Systems Diagrams

The primary tool of systems thinking is a *systems diagram.* These identify the inter-relationships that exist between phenomena in a system. Systems diagrams are comprised of reinforcing and balancing feedback loops that portray the causal effects that variables within a system have on each other and on the overall system. Feedback loops portray these effects across both space and time and can attend to internal dynamics as well, depending on the person creating the diagram. For a superb introduction to systems thinking and systems diagrams, we refer you to Peter Senge's (1990) book, *The Fifth Discipline.* More detailed application can be found in *The Fifth Discipline Fieldbook,* written by Senge (1994) and others.

In systems thinking language, the unique relationships among variables in a system create an underlying dynamic "structure." All systems have underlying dynamic structures that "cause" the behavior of the system. Systems thinking suggests that if leaders want to change the organization's behavior, then they must identify and alter these underlying structures. Furthermore, systems thinking suggests that within any system there are "leverage points," places where small, well-focused actions will produce larger desired results. Applying leverage is the concept of "maximum gain for minimum effort." Systems diagrams, which outline the organization's underlying dynamic structure, assist systems thinkers to identify the leverage points for change.

For change leaders attending to all twenty-one dimensions, identifying the leverage points for change is perhaps the greatest value of systems thinking and systems mapping. These leverage points will identify the critical content and people changes, revealing the most beneficial changes to the strategy, structure, systems, technology, or processes, as well as the required changes to mindset and culture. All change leaders should become familiar with systems diagrams, as they can be invaluable aids in identifying *what* must change. Their limitation is that they do not provide insight about *how* the change might occur. That is the job of a change process model.

Change Process Models

Change process models are tools of conscious process thinking. They are both action oriented and results producing. They organize the activities of the change process so the transformation's desired outcomes are achieved over time. Change process models possess varying degrees of effectiveness, based on how accurately and completely they reflect the actual process dynamics of transformation (the twenty-one dimensions). Figure 7.3 (page 169) in Chapter Seven portrays the phase level of our own Change Process Model for Leading Conscious Transformation.

A systems diagram can show change leaders what levers to pull to produce maximum change, whereas a comprehensive change process model organizes the activities to actually pull the levers. In other words, systems diagrams build *knowledge* about the systems dynamics, whereas a change process model organizes *action* to alter the systems dynamics. Each tool needs the other to deliver its full benefit.

There are a number of systems analysis tools that have been developed over the years to map work-flow processes. These should not be confused with change process models. "Process mapping," as used in quality and continuous process improvement, is perhaps the most well-known of these tools.

Process maps denote the chronological sequence of steps within discrete processes. They can be highly detailed or extremely generic, as in W. Edwards Deming's famous process, "plan, do, study, act." First, you plan, then you do, then you study what occurred, then you take subsequent action. You don't take the second action until you have completed the first (note again the influence of project thinking).

Process maps are often confused with systems diagrams, although they are extremely different. In a systems diagram, a change in any variable will change all variables within the dynamic system. In other words, systems diagrams demonstrate the interrelated dynamics across all mapped components throughout *time*. A process diagram, on the other hand, is a snapshot of how a process functions at a *point in time*. A process map will not show the system impacts over time of altering a step in the process; process maps can only reveal the sequential relationship of individual steps. Systems diagrams and process maps can be used synergistically, but their application should not be confused.

While process maps define the *prescribed sequential steps* in an isolated organizational process that will be *stable, consistent, and repeated over time*, a change process model provides a *suggested* plan of action for how to *change* an organization over time. Process maps promote stability and consistency; change process models drive change.

These distinctions are critical. Transformation is dynamic and unpredictable. You cannot map its process sequentially. In fact, you cannot map (predict) its process with any level of certainty. Therefore, a change process model should not prescribe linear actions. Instead, it should offer a general guidance system for organizing actions that will catalyze the transformation toward desired outcomes. A change process model must be flexible and adaptable in real time to the emerging dynamics as they arise.

Process maps, systems diagrams, and change process models all have their place in transformation. Which of these tools are used, and how, should be a function of what is required. Most often, however, the change leader's style determines the tool.

The Impact of Change Leadership Styles on Process Design and Facilitation

Transformation, ultimately, is the journey from where an organization is to where it chooses to be, when the change required to get there is so significant that it requires the people and culture of the organization to "transform," and the journey must begin before you can fully identify where "there" is.

Change leadership is the function of leading an organization through this journey. Change leaders are responsible both for designing the process of this journey and for overseeing that process as it unfolds. We refer to these change leadership responsibilities as process design and process facilitation.

Process Design and Facilitation

Process design governs the advance planning and creation of any process, whereas process facilitation pertains to real-time oversight and execution of that preliminary design. Process design is akin to the "game plan" that coaches of a sports team prepare *before* the game; it is how they want the game to go. Process facilitation entails the real-time play calling *during* the game; it requires the coaches to respond in the moment to what is actually happening on the field. Similarly, an architect uses process design to *conceive* a custom home, whereas the builder uses process facilitation to *construct* the house to both the plan's specification and the client's changing desires.

Throughout this book, we have referred to the need for change leaders to attend to the *actual* dynamics and requirements of transformation. Conscious process thinking enables change leaders to discover and see these dynamics and requirements. *Process design* is the preliminary strategy that they develop to attend to these dynamics, whereas *process facilitation* refers to change leaders' implementation of their process design, while responding to the actual dynamics and requirements that spontaneously arise. Let's now explore how a change leader's style impacts process design and process facilitation.

Three Change Leadership Styles

In our years of consulting to organizations in change, we have witnessed innumerable change leadership styles. The range of these styles delineate a continuum represented by three basic styles: (1) controlling, (2) facilitating, and (3) self-organizing (see Figure 6.1). The controlling style comes right out of the Industrial Mindset, while both the facilitative and the self-organizing styles are indicative of the Emerging Mindset.

Figure 6.1. Continuum of Change Leadership Styles

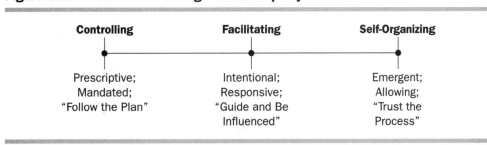

Controlling	Facilitating	Self-Organizing
Prescriptive; Mandated; "Follow the Plan"	Intentional; Responsive; "Guide and Be Influenced"	Emergent; Allowing; "Trust the Process"

Controlling Change Leadership Style

Controlling change leaders tend to use project management tools to design their change process according to a prescribed sequential methodology, then install or implement that plan with little or no variation. The process design phase is mostly dictated by the methodology, whereas the process facilitation phase is simply the rigid execution of the plan as designed.

As you might expect, controlling change leaders usually attend only to external reality and neglect people and cultural forces and needs. With leaders using this style in charge, the transformation journey is usually filled with stress, conflict, and confusion. The inflexibility of this change leadership style just doesn't fit the dynamic nature of transformation. The only situation we know of where leaders adopting this style have any hope of succeeding in transformation is when all four of the following variables are in place: (1) The leader is extremely charismatic; (2) the organization is in crisis; (3) a critical mass of people understand the urgency; and (4) people trust the leader enough to follow his or her "orders."

Facilitating Change Leadership Style

Facilitative change leaders use a comprehensive change process model to design their change process in advance; then, during process facilitation, they consciously alter the implementation of their design as the emerging dynamics require. Therefore, their change process model must support clear, up-front design, as well as flexible implementation.

Because they expect to course correct their design based on what they learn in real time, facilitative change leaders listen carefully for information coming from their people, organization, or marketplace that suggests how to better facilitate the transformation. For this reason, they encourage open exchange of information and high participation; to this end, they orient more to asking the right questions than to providing answers. Facilitative leaders attend to both internal and external realities as they design and facilitate their transformation process and are willing to alter the plans of either. They place significant attention on setting the conditions for success up front so the process can roll out in the best possible way.

Self-Organizing Change Leadership Style

Self-organizing change leaders do not use a structured methodology, but allow the transformation process to organize itself, more or less. Self-organizing change leaders do not attempt to control or even heavily influence the change process, either by establishing a preliminary process design or by facilitating. Instead, self-organizing change leaders allow both the design and facilitation of the transformation process to emerge directly from the organization.

Self-organizing change leaders use various change tools to establish certain favorable conditions in their organizations. They create shared vision throughout the organization. They build common understanding of the case for change, as well as foster mass understanding of the organization's current systems dynamics that are causing its current behavior. They remove barriers to information generation and exchange so that the entire organization can be as aware as possible of its current state, its desired future state, and what is supporting or blocking progress. And they provide resources and support as needed. The rest is left up to the organization. Self-organizing change leaders nurture the conditions for transformation within the organization, but allow the actual design and facilitation of the process of change to emerge from the organization. If the process sputters, they help the organization see the breakdown, but they do not jump in and attempt to fix the problem as a controlling change leader would. For self-organizing leaders, solutions are the organization's responsibility.

Is One Style Best?

In 1982, Ken Blanchard and Paul Hersey introduced the now popular concept of Situational Leadership in their book *Management of Organizational Behavior.* These authors say that leaders need to adopt the leadership style that is best suited for the situation they face. As the situation changes, so should their leadership style. In change leadership, the requirement is the same. There is no one correct change leadership style. Change leaders must alter their style to suit the type, scope, and intent of their change initiatives. For example, in developmental or transitional change, perhaps the controlling or facilitating styles would offer the best fit; in transformation, the facilitating or self-organizing styles might serve best. The best style for your situation may actually be a hybrid of all three styles.

However, generally speaking, we believe that the facilitative change leadership style best fits the majority of transformation efforts in *today's* business environment. First, the facilitative style reflects and incorporates the insights of the Emerging Mindset, so transformation processes designed and run with it will demonstrate a shift from the organization's old way of operating and, therefore, model a new way. Facilitated transformation processes reflect the ten operating principles. Second, although this style may be a stretch for many leaders because it requires them to break out of their linear, project-thinking orientation and temper their control tendencies, it is achievable by most. Third, the level of organizational change readiness and capacity required by the facilitative style is attainable, even for many of today's hierarchical command and control organizations.

We believe that the self-organizing style is the wave of the *future,* although a number of change leaders are experimenting successfully with it now. This style most fully embodies the Emerging Mindset and has the greatest hope of actualizing the maximum human potential while creating the conditions in the organization to respond most effectively and quickly to dynamic changes in the marketplace. However, not many of today's organizations are yet ready for the self-organizing style.

The self-organizing style requires an evolution of leadership and employee skill. The self-organizing style requires a very talented and conscious process thinking change leader who is willing and able to share power, as well as an organization with aware and responsible employees who possess self-mastery and personal change skills themselves.

The self-organizing style also requires a different organizational design than currently exists in most organizations. Structure must be flatter and more flexible. Decision-making processes must be streamlined. Strategic planning processes must be expanded to include greater participation. Information technology systems must provide universal access to knowledge and information throughout the organization.

Leaders, employees, and organizations are evolving, and in the next twenty years will develop the capacity for the self-organizing style. In the meantime, the facilitative style and its tool, a change process model, can deliver the transformations required.

By providing guidance, a comprehensive change process model can assist leaders and employees to develop the critical change skills and competencies. It can support them to integrate their content and people changes. It can keep them attending to all twenty-one critical dimensions of process so they can design appropriate interventions as required. It can ensure that they consciously design and facilitate their transformation based on the Emerging Mindset perspective, applying all ten operating principles. A solid change process model can alert leaders and employees to transformational dynamics they might otherwise overlook and reinforce continued attendance to their own personal transformation. In short, a comprehensive change process model can support leaders and employees to become aware of what is required in transformation so they do not fall back into their reactive, controlling, project-management-based approaches.

Use Exhibit 6.1 to assess your change leadership style, both your existing style and the style you think would be best for leading your transformation, if different. The exhibit displays the three change leadership styles and eight areas of focus as they apply to each style. Read down one column at a time. Place an X in the left-hand response box below the wording that best describes your existing change leadership behaviors. Answer the questions based on how you lead or consult when you are in your normal state of awareness or on autopilot. Mark only one left-hand box per column. The resulting pattern of Xs will reveal your dominant change leadership style.

Then, go back through the assessment, placing an O in the right-hand response boxes in the columns to represent your *desired* change leadership behaviors—those you think or feel would best serve the transformation you are leading. The resulting pattern of Os will either reinforce your existing change leadership style or highlight the style you would like to adopt. Any differences between the patterns highlights critical areas for your personal development.

Summary

In this chapter, we defined the term *process* as "the natural or intentional unfolding of continuous events, within all dimensions of reality, toward a desired outcome." We said that all twenty-one dimensions of conscious transformation are continually "in process" and that all dimensions are interdependent. We stressed that any one of them can surface as a significant force within an organization's transformation, making it imperative that change leaders attend to the process dynamics of all twenty-one dimensions.

We differentiated among three different thinking orientations: project thinking, systems thinking, and conscious process thinking—and described the tools that each orientation relies on to produce change results. In particular, we identified the differences among project management methodologies, systems diagrams, process maps, and change process models.

We distinguished among three different types of change leadership style—controlling, facilitating, and self-organizing. We made a strong case for the facilitative style, and its tool, a change process model, as most appropriate for most of today's leaders, employees, and organizations. We explained the change leadership functions of process design and process facilitation, suggesting that facilitative change leaders must consciously design their change process, then consciously facilitate it, as emerging dynamics warrant. We suggested further that the operating principles of conscious transformation as outlined in the last chapter govern both process design and process facilitation.

In the next chapter, we will continue to explore the critical requirements of a comprehensive change process model and introduce our own nine-phase *Change Process Model for Leading Conscious Transformation.*

Exhibit 6.1. Assessing Your Change Leadership Style

	Orientation	How Future State Is Designed	Treatment of Information	View of Process
Controlling	I see myself as the boss.	I decide, sometimes with a little input from my direct reports.	I control information and share it on a need-to-know basis. I don't like bad news.	The plan dictates all action; I expect very little deviation.
Facilitating	I see myself as the coach.	I ensure clear design requirements and encourage appropriate participation.	I openly exchange information through planned communications. I am open to hearing bad news.	The plan guides action and is continuously corrected as new information is discovered.
Self-Organizing	I see myself as a coach, one of many resources in the organization.	I support conditions and processes for the future state design to emerge.	I support my organization to share all information across levels freely. I seek out bad news to learn.	The process is emergent. We figure out the right action in the right time.

Openness to Feedback	View of Structures	View of Measurement	View of Personal Change
Feedback disrupts me. I don't really want it.	I use structures to maintain control; hierarchical ones are best.	I require the measurement of progress, using strict quantifiable criteria.	I don't think personal change is necessary or relevant. I am too busy with more important matters.
I accept feedback and realize it is important, even though it is sometimes uncomfortable.	I use structures to support change and foster participation; I see them as temporary and can work with flat, networked, or hierarchical structures.	I can see the value of measurement for learning and course correcting.	Personal change is required to make me more effective.
I seek feedback, comfortable or not, because it is essential to my, and our, success.	Structures are useful tools to support the process. They come and go as needed.	I use measures primarily to focus attention and never see measures as having objective truth.	Transforming my consciousness is the source of my success and fulfillment.

Change Process Models

TRAVELING INTO NEW TERRITORY CENTURIES AGO must have been extremely challenging and scary, to say the least. The first pioneers had no maps, no way to know whether food, water, or hostile enemies were around the next bend or over the next mountain. They assumed that opportunity lay ahead, but had no way of knowing whether their route was going to get them there, wherever "there" was.

Navigating organizational transformation over the past few decades has been a similar experience for adventuresome leaders and consultants alike. Change leader pioneers have had few maps and little reconnaissance information to support their journey. Most of them traveled alone.

A roadmap is invaluable for traveling in new territory. Transformational change leaders especially need a roadmap to guide their journey as they move beyond the territory of managing developmental and transitional change into leading transformational change.

In the last chapter, we began the introduction of change process models which, when designed properly, are in fact roadmaps for transformation. In this chapter, we further explore process models, differentiate them from change frameworks, and explain why they must be "thinking disciplines," rather than prescriptions for action. We also introduce the notion of "fullstream" transformation, which any comprehensive change process model must embrace. We conclude the chapter with a conceptual overview of our own nine-phase *Change Process Model for Leading Conscious Transformation*. When we speak generically about change process models, we will use lower case letters; when we speak specifically about our own Change Process Model, we will use initial capitalization.

We have developed our Change Process Model as the result of taking numerous transformational journeys with our clients over the past twenty-five years. Because we have repeatedly scouted the territory as we looked for passable routes, our journeys have revealed much about the transformational terrain. First, we know that the trip is full of humility; success is never guaranteed, even if you do have a roadmap. Second, we know that a roadmap is highly beneficial; specific obstacles always seem to be present around certain bends in the river, and clear paths can be repeatedly found in similar circumstances. Having a roadmap has not taken the mystery out of the journey, but it certainly has made finding a workable route more likely.

Change Process Methodologies

Change process methodologies are the methods, rules, or guidelines for facilitating any change process. Any effective *transformational* change methodology must accomplish the outcomes of transformation while building essential and lasting change competencies in the people and organization. A sample list of the focus, activities, and competencies of an effective transformational change methodology includes:

- The understanding that transformation is a multi-dimensional process;
- Conscious change process design: The knowledge and skills for designing a transformational change strategy and process that integrates content and people changes;
- Conscious change process facilitation: The knowledge and skills for learning from and course correcting the change strategy and process throughout implementation;

- Attention to the leaders, the workforce, and all relevant stakeholders;

- The establishment of the required infrastructures, roles, and conditions for success;

- Strategies to deal effectively with the people dynamics of change, individually and collectively, including changing the existing mindset and culture and helping people through their natural reactions to the change; and

- Strategies to manage, support, and permeate the boundaries between the organization's ongoing operation and the rollout of the change.

Clearly, some kind of change model is needed to assist leaders to address all of the activities and competencies of transformation.

A scan of the literature and the practices of organization development and change management reveals many models designed to help organizations improve how they change and grow. These models seem to fall into two categories: *frameworks* and *process models.* The majority of models available today are frameworks. Some speak to process, but at varying levels of specificity. Both frameworks and process models are valuable for leading change, but a process model is absolutely essential to leading transformation. Let's explore their differences.

Change Frameworks vs. Change Process Models

Change frameworks present the types or categories of topics requiring leadership attention to effect change. For example, McKinsey's 7-S Framework (Peters & Waterman, 1982), Weisbord's Six Box Model (1978), Nadler and Tushman's Congruence Model (1977), Miles' Framework for Leading Corporate Transformation (1997), and our own Three Elements of a Comprehensive Change Strategy Model (Ackerman Anderson & Anderson, 1996) that identifies content, people, and process, are all good examples.

In general, frameworks offer an organizing construct for what to pay attention to when undergoing change. Think of them as handy catalog indexes for selecting information and topics relevant to change. They can be useful as planning tools and checklists. For example, if you were redesigning your organization, you might choose to use the 7-S Framework (Figure 7.1) to help you identify what key areas require attention.

Figure 7.1. McKinsey's 7-S Framework

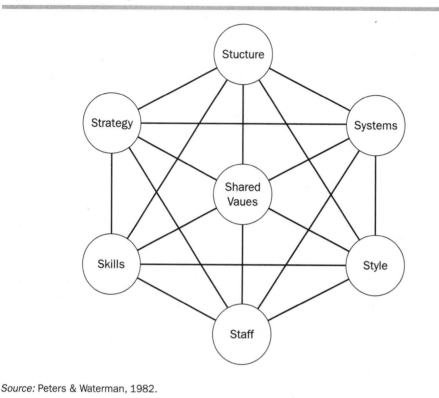

Source: Peters & Waterman, 1982.

The model gives an accurate, albeit static representation of seven core elements of an organization and portrays that they are all interconnected. As useful as the framework might be for pointing to the most critical areas requiring redesign, it does not tell you what to do to accomplish this redesign. It provides no guidance about how to sequence the items you may need to attend to nor does it explain what tangible actions to take to accomplish each item. By itself, the 7-S Framework is insufficient for guiding the *process* of redesigning the organization because it applies a still camera's view to a continuous process, much like incomplete systems maps do. Frameworks can be great educational tools, but have little application in the field. For that, you need a more dynamic model, a change process model.

Although change frameworks are generally static, change process models demonstrate action, movement, and flow. They offer guidance on what to *do* to accomplish change and, *generally*, in what order. Think of process models as roadmaps for action that provide a potential path to follow for designing and implementing your future state. Because transformation requires getting from where you are to where you want to be, having a roadmap that portrays the *process* of the journey is essential.

Currently available process models include Conner's Cycle of Change (1998), Nadler's Cycle of Change (1998), and Kotter's Eight Stage Process of Creating Major Change (1996). Each provides unique process guidance, and several also function like frameworks by listing many important topics requiring attention. Kotter's model, in particular, appears to us to be a hybrid. The first four phases denote a process flow (one stage leads to the next), while the last four specify areas to nurture and give attention (as in a framework model).

From our perspective, the majority of current change process models are either too general or reflect only a partial picture of what is required to lead transformational change. Some focus exclusively on human transformation and neglect any attention to business content. Many more do the reverse, attending heavily to business and organizational imperatives but placing inadequate attention on human dynamics and needs.

Some are too conceptual and neglect guidance at the operational level of getting things done. For example, "Plan, Do, Study, and Act" may represent a process, yet is of minimal help to leaders faced with the complex drama of orchestrating transformational change. More pragmatic guidance is necessary. Other models we have investigated focus only on implementation and neglect design. Others are based on ill-conceived concepts of transformation, that is, are too prescriptive for the dynamic realities of transformation or attend only to external realities and neglect the internal world of the human psyche.

Leaders and consultants need an effective and comprehensive change process model that is fit for transformation. Such a model must attend to and integrate people and content needs. It must be both conceptual and pragmatic, providing clear guidance about how to truly plan and oversee the action required to create desired outcomes. It should portray how change actually takes place, giving leaders a map of the territory for tailoring, supporting, and accelerating their actual change efforts. Leaders need a change process model that expands their thinking about both the internal and external dynamics of transformation, one that helps them observe what is actually occurring in their live transformation. Mostly, this model must provide "informed guesses" for designing in advance what has to occur for the transformation to succeed, as well as insight about how to course correct when unexpected circumstances arise—as they will.

A successful change process model must adequately attend to all twenty-one dimensions of effective change leadership. It must help leaders to view transformation through the eyes of the Emerging Mindset and, most importantly, reflect the ten operating principles of conscious transformation. It must support leaders to think and act congruently with these principles. And, of greater importance, it must be a *thinking discipline* rather than a prescription for action, and it must be *full-stream*. We will explain the notion of thinking disciplines first, then address the full-stream concept.

The Change Process Model As a Thinking Discipline

This is perhaps the most significant message we can convey about ours, or anyone's, guidance system for transformation:

> Your roadmap must be a process model fit for transformation, not a project management methodology. Your roadmap can and should guide action, but not mandate it. It can and should inform process design decisions, but not prescribe them. It can and should organize your plan, but not rigidify it. In other words, your change process model can be structured, but it must accommodate the evolving, multi-dimensional *process* nature of transformation.

Having said that, let's not throw out the baby with the bath water. Just because your change is transformational does not mean that you cannot use a structured guidance system. You can and should. The key is that the guidance system must help to discipline your thinking. It must call you to attend to dynamics that you would otherwise neglect and, in doing so, make you more conscious! By all means, do not allow your guidance system to take over your planning process without your first thinking through what is required given the complex dynamics you face. That would take your conscious awareness completely out of the game, which would forfeit any possibility of success. Remember that *the primary purpose of any change process model must be to increase your conscious awareness for better process design and real-time process facilitation.*

Transformation demands that you participate and co-create with your emerging dynamics, but it does not demand that you forego any structured support for how to expand your conscious awareness of the process dynamics at play and how to attend to them. A good change process model should assist you in this regard.

Transformation As a Fullstream Process

When leaders first hear the wake-up call that a transformational change is required, the thinking, planning, and communicating that takes place all have implications for how the change will occur and how employees will receive it. A comprehensive change process model must attend to designing the transformation from the initial wake-up call through achievement of the desired state. We call this entire process "fullstream transformation" (see Figure 7.2).

Figure 7.2. Fullstream Transformation Model

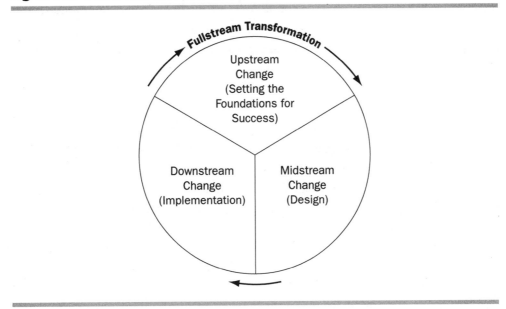

Transformation, as a continuous process, has an upstream component, a midstream component, and a downstream component, all of which need to be designed and led consciously for the transformation to succeed. The *upstream* stage is oriented to planning and setting the foundations for success. The *midstream* stage is focused on designing the desired state, while the *downstream* stage is about implementation. All change process models that are not fullstream neglect at least one of these critical stages, causing the transformation to fall short of expectations. We will describe what is in each stage, as perceived through the eyes of the facilitative change leadership style, and highlight some of the common challenges that occur within them. Keep in mind that controlling or self-organizing change leaders would treat the process differently.

Upstream Change

The upstream stage of transformation, setting the foundations for success, begins with hearing the wake-up call. In this stage, change leaders assess their organization's capacity to succeed in the change, as well as become clear about the case for change. They decide who is leading the effort, develop their change strategy, and identify conditions and infrastructures needed to support the successful achievement of the desired outcome. They develop their communication and participation plans, as well as other key support functions. This part of upstream change is the leaders' opportunity to get their heads, hearts, and hands aligned before engaging the rest of the organization in the change. Without such unity and commitment, the change, and its leadership, are usually seen by employees as disorganized and incompetent, which creates a significant hurdle to overcome. Building leadership alignment up-front sets the ideal conditions for positive employee involvement throughout the change.

Also during the upstream stage, the workforce is fully engaged in the transformation. Employees are informed about the rationale for the transformation and, in many cases, actually help build the case for change. They are fully supported to participate in the planning efforts early in the change process. This builds buy-in and commitment and sets the stage for minimal downstream resistance. Initiating the transformation in ways that are positive and well-received is a critical aspect of the upstream stage. All of this work *precedes* the actual design of the desired future state or the "solution." In other words, employees become involved long before design and implementation.

The upstream stage is where the climate, commitment, and runway for the entire change are established. It includes critical leadership decisions that are the primary acceleration rockets for the effort. The time and attention this stage takes pays off exponentially throughout the remainder of the change process. It models the operating principle, "Go slow to go fast," and it also gives leaders the opportunity to walk their talk of the change right from the start, modeling their desired culture "as if it already existed."

Midstream Change

The midstream stage of change is when the *actual* design of the desired state occurs. The design is developed, clarified, tested, and refined. Its impact is studied, and plans are created to pace and coordinate its implementation accurately. All of the conditions, structures, systems, and policies decided in the upstream stage are tailored and established to help prepare and support the organization for implementation. More readiness is built through participation, and the organization's capacity to succeed in the change is further developed.

Many organizations become stuck in midstream change, spending untold dollars, resources, and hours solely on the design of their desired future state. When this occurs, it is often because they are leaning too far toward a controlling style and place exclusive priority on developing the "right" answer, the right content of their change. These are usually high-compliance organizations, where little significant action occurs unless there is a very high certainty or predictability of success. Whether the organization develops the design using internal expertise or an external consulting firm does not seem to matter.

The over-focus on design can create an under-focus on implementation. By the time the design is finalized, the leaders may be in such a rush to get the new state in place that they save little time to plan adequately for its implementation. Sometimes, the organization has run out of budget for downstream change activities as well. It's as if the writing of the perfect script for the change gets all of the leaders' attention and there is no energy given to what it takes to actually perform the play! In this all too common scenario, the leaders have focused on design or midstream change, at the expense of implementation or downstream change. And to further complicate matters in this scenario, we usually find that such leaders have also neglected the upstream stage as well.

Downstream Change

The downstream stage includes implementation, change integration, and learning about and course correcting the new state. Skill training about how to operate in the new state occurs, as does building best change practices and dismantling the change infrastructure when it is no longer needed. This is also the time of celebration during which support for making the transformation a success is officially acknowledged.

A common mistake frequently occurs in this stage, especially when the pace of change has been mandated and is unrealistic. In this scenario, leaders rush into implementation before they have adequately identified and created the upstream conditions for success or before they have adequately completed their desired-state designs and tested them for feasibility. This makes implementation extremely difficult. As implementation begins, the need for the neglected yet necessary upstream and midstream work becomes apparent. Leaders are forced to stop implementation in order to clarify what is required for success, further flesh out the details of the desired state, or study its impacts. Employees become resistant, as they feel jerked around by leaders' poor planning and the "stop and go" dynamic it creates.

In the early 1990s, when change management was first gaining speed as a legitimate practice, we performed an informal research study to identify what "change management" meant to leaders and what they wanted and were ready to hear about leading change. We found that most leaders believed that change management meant the *implementation* of a desired outcome that had previously been designed and the need to overcome employee resistance. They recognized the need for change management only when they couldn't put their good solutions into action successfully, due largely to workforce opposition or emotional upheaval.

When leaders want change management to *start* with implementation, it is no wonder that their well-intentioned efforts flounder! With no preliminary foundations to assist the organization to receive or participate in the change, and with what is likely an inadequate design of their desired state because of their rush to implement, leaders' hopes that change management or organization development will salvage a shaky or resisted implementation are unrealistic. The seeds of a successful change are sown in the upstream and midstream stages. Implementation is essential, yet it is only one of the three necessary stages of the transformation process. Furthermore, when good upstream and midstream work are accomplished, implementation goes more smoothly, as employees are much more committed to creating a desired future state that they understand and have helped design. We believe that change methodologies that focus heavily on implementation planning and overcoming employee resistance exist only because leaders tend to neglect the required upstream and midstream change activities.

Although the "fullstream transformation model" offers a conceptual overview of the process of change, it has little value in actually guiding a live change effort because it is too general. The model's value is only in introducing leaders to an expanded view of all of the stages of the process of change. To actually lead transformation successfully, a more developed change process model is required.

The Nine-Phase Change Process Model

The nine-phase Change Process Model for Leading Conscious Transformation, shown in Figure 7.3, attends to what we believe is required of a comprehensive change process model fit for transformation.

Figure 7.3. The Nine-Phase Change Process Model for Leading Conscious Transformation

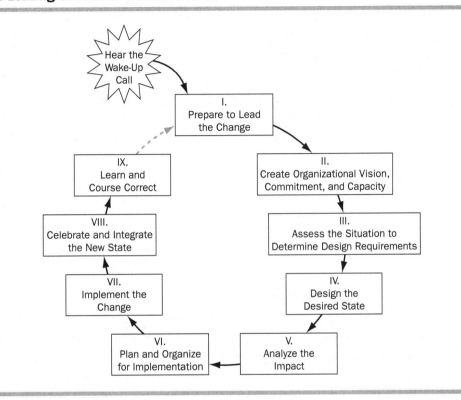

The model represents a fullstream roadmap for getting your organization from where it is to where it wants to be. The nine phases represent the generic process of how change takes place in organizations over time. The model integrates the change strategy elements of content, people, and process and attends to the twenty-one dimensions.

We have been working with the Change Process Model for twenty years. In the early 1980s, we used it in a simpler form for guiding transitional change. As we learned more about transformational change and the Emerging Mindset, we re-designed the model specifically to address the process dynamics of transformation. In its current state of development, the model assists leaders to take a conscious approach to leading transformation.

Although designed for transformational change, the Change Process Model can be tailored for all types of change, as well as any magnitude of change effort. Smaller, less complex transitional changes require selective tailoring of the activities in the model. Even more tailoring is required for developmental change applications, as the model attends to much more than is required in most developmental changes. Quite frankly, such a comprehensive change process model is seldom called for in developmental change.

The model graphically represents the inherent logic and flow of the key phases of transformation. You may, however, mistakenly interpret the sequential graphic to mean that you must complete one phase before you proceed to the next. In actual practice, transformation is not linear and you may be in two, three, or even four phases simultaneously. You may do the work of some phases in parallel with doing the work of other phases as your situation dictates. Remember that this model is a thinking discipline, not a project management methodology. Therefore, you can combine phases however you choose, given your circumstances.

In a complex transformation, the enterprise is often going through an overarching nine-phase change process while simultaneously, individual change initiatives engage in their own processes within the overall transformation. Therefore, different change initiatives, business units, or regions of the enterprise may be in different phases. The key, of course, is to ensure adequate integration so that all individual initiatives support the overarching change of the enterprise. When each change effort is using the same change process model, integration becomes much easier. The reality of the complex, nonlinear dynamics of the model in action is shown in Figure 7.4.

Structure of the Change Process Model

The model incorporates the fullstream transformation model (see Figure 7.5) in that three of the nine phases represent upstream, three midstream, and three downstream processes. Phases I to III are the upstream stage (setting the foundations for success), Phases IV to VI comprises the midstream stage (design), and Phases VII through IX denotes the downstream stage (implementation).

There are several levels of guidance available in the model, from conceptual to very detailed. Depending on your need, you can customize the application of the model to any level of detail.

The most conceptual level is the general description of the nine phases as shown in Figure 7.3. Each phase is further organized into major activities, as outlined in Figure 7.6. Each activity is achieved through focused tasks. The tasks for each activity all have deliverables, which, at the most operational level, are accomplished through a series of suggested work steps.

Figure 7.4. The Change Process Model in Action

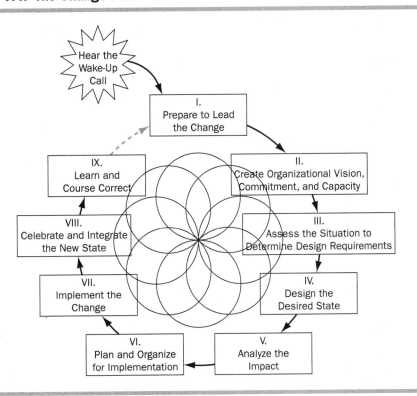

We have structured the material in this way—phase, activity, task, work steps—for ease of use for line managers who are familiar with similarly structured project management methodologies. This structure gives them a familiar language and organizing construct. It also provides the greatest versatility for the various people who use the model, be they executives who need only the conceptual phase level or change process leaders and consultants who benefit from the greater detail.

The subject of our companion book, *The Change Leader's Roadmap*, is how to use the nine-phase model, so we will provide no further detail here. We introduce the Change Process Model to demonstrate that a comprehensive one must be broad (fullstream), deep (conceptual to pragmatic), and adaptable.

Figure 7.5. The Change Process Model As a Fullstream Process

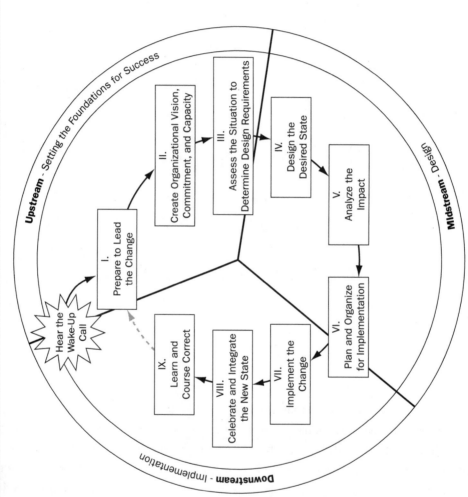

Figure 7.6. Change Process Model—Activity Level

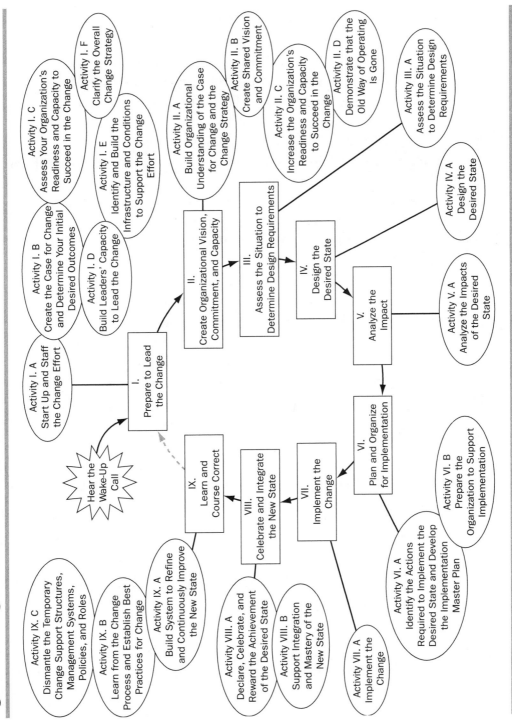

There Is No Cookbook for Transformation!

The Change Process Model was designed to benefit both leaders and consultants. However, unconsciously applying the model can be hazardous to either. This is because, first, the detail, logic, and structure of the Change Process Model might create the impression that it is a cookbook for how to succeed at transformation. The structure of the model may give the illusion that transformation can be carefully managed, sequenced, and controlled. As we have already said, this is not possible! There is no cookbook for transformational change. Anyone using the Change Process Model must remember that it is a thinking discipline, not a prescription for action.

Second, we created the Change Process Model to be as complete and comprehensive as possible. We included everything that we have discovered to be critical in leading and consulting to transformation. That thoroughness is both a strength and a potential weakness of the model.

Remember, the Change Process Model, in all its comprehensiveness, is simply designed to support you as you consciously ask which of its many activities are critical for *your* transformation's success. The application of the model must be tailored, *always,* to the outcomes, magnitude, change leadership style, pacing requirements, and resource constraints unique to your situation.

In any given transformation effort, we suggest that you consider all of what is offered in the model and then select *only* the work that is appropriate to your change effort and what will help you guide and accelerate your change. You should skip activities that have been completed or are of marginal or no value to your situation. Furthermore, you should combine tasks or run them in parallel whenever possible to achieve multiple deliverables simultaneously. And of course, you will always need to decide for yourself how you will actually design each chosen task in real time. Customization is key.

Comparing Your Experience with Other Change Models

When teaching the Change Process Model to seasoned change leaders and consultants, we have found it useful to have them compare their experience with other models with using the nine-phase Change Process Model. Our intention is always to expand their view of how to lead transformation effectively and add to their existing expertise, not replace it. Exhibit 7.1 offers a series of questions to assist you in this comparison.

Exhibit 7.1. Comparing Other Change Models with the Change Process Model

1. What change frameworks are you familiar with or have you used?

2. What other change process models are you familiar with or have you used?

3. What aspects of each of the above models fall under each of the three stages of the Fullstream Transformation Model?

   ☐ Upstream stage:

   ☐ Midstream stage:

   ☐ Downstream stage:

4. Do aspects of any of the models address issues not within the three stages of change? If so, what are they, and how would you describe them?

5. For each of the above models, which focus your attention on building a change strategy for the overall transformation?

6. Which focus your attention on the **content** of the transformation?

7. Which focus on the **people** dynamics of the transformation?

**Exhibit 7.1. Comparing Other Change Models
with the Change Process Model, Cont'd**

8. Of the change process models you listed, how would you compare their guidance against the nine phases and all of the activities of the Change Process Model? Check the activities within each phase that you feel are adequately covered in the models you currently use:

Phase I: Prepare to Lead the Change

☐ Activity I.A Start Up and Staff the Change Effort

☐ Activity I.B Create the Case for Change and Determine Your Initial Desired Outcomes

☐ Activity I.C Assess the Organization's Readiness and Capacity to Succeed in the Change

☐ Activity I.D Build Leaders' Capacity to Lead the Change

☐ Activity I.E Identify and Build the Infrastructure and Conditions to Support the Change Effort

☐ Activity I.F Clarify the Overall Change Strategy

Phase II: Create Organizational Vision, Commitment, and Capacity

☐ Activity II.A Build Organizational Understanding of the Case for Change and the Change Strategy

☐ Activity II.B Create Shared Vision and Commitment

☐ Activity II.C Increase the Organization's Readiness and Capacity to Succeed in the Change

☐ Activity II.D Demonstrate that the Old Way of Operating Is Gone

Phase III: Assess the Situation to Determine Design Requirements

☐ Activity III.A Assess the Situation to Determine Design Requirements

Phase IV: Design the Desired State

☐ Activity IV.A Design the Desired State

Phase V: Analyze the Impact

☐ Activity V.A. Analyze the Impacts of the Desired State

**Exhibit 7.1. Comparing Other Change Models
with the Change Process Model, Cont'd**

Phase VI: Plan and Organize for Implementation

☐ Activity VI.A Identify the Actions Required to Implement the Desired State and Develop the Implementation Master Plan

☐ Activity VI.B Prepare the Organization to Support Implementation

Phase VII: Implement the Change

☐ Activity VII.A Implement the Change

Phase VIII: Celebrate and Integrate the New State

☐ Activity VIII.A Declare, Celebrate, and Reward the Achievement of the Desired State

☐ Activity VIII.B Support Integration and Mastery of the New State

Phase IX: Learn and Course Correct

☐ Activity IX.A Build a System to Refine and Continuously Improve the New State

☐ Activity IX.B Learn from the Change Process and Establish Best Practices for Change

☐ Activity IX.C Dismantle the Temporary Change Support Structures, Management Systems, Policies, and Roles

9. For this question, set aside your attention to any change framework or change process model, including the Change Process Model. What does your *experience* say about what is needed to lead the process of transformation consciously and effectively *in real time*? What guidance would you want to make sure was heeded?

Summary

Transformation is a complex, multi-dimensional process that can be greatly served by a structured change process model to discipline your thinking and help you to remain conscious of all of the dynamics to which you must attend. Such a model must honor the process nature of transformation and provide a roadmap for navigating its complexities. Change frameworks, while valuable to identify critical areas of attention, do not suffice for designing and leading the *process* of transformation. A change process model is required.

This concludes our discussion of conscious process thinking. In Section Four, we explore how the evolution of change has impacted the role of managers and leaders and demonstrate how being a conscious transformational change leader denotes leaders' next level of growth and development.

Section Four
Conscious Transformational Leadership

Developing Conscious Change Leaders

(M)UCH LIKE THE PROCESS OF TRANSFORMATION ITSELF, we have taken a long journey to get to this point in our discussion. In the last three sections, we have defined conscious transformation, explored mindset as the key leverage point for transformation, and introduced a multi-dimensional process orientation for leading transformation. In this section, we turn to the development of change leaders.

This chapter focuses on developing leaders into change leaders. As a foundation, we provide an overview of the evolution of managers into change leaders. Then we delve into the arenas of development for conscious transformational leadership, clarify the design principles for creating a change leadership development curriculum, and offer a template for your consideration.

The Evolution of the Leader's Role

An exploration of how the leader's role has evolved in organizations provides a valuable backdrop for our discussion. This review provides a historical context of the expanding demands placed on leaders and the skills required of them. Leaders weren't always referred to as leaders. As we see it, their role evolved through four stages, from manager to leader to change manager to change leader—what we think of as a "conscious transformational leader." (See Figure 8.1 for an outline of the evolution of the leader's role.) Because that name is such a mouthful, we just say "change leader" or "conscious change leader." However, remember that change leadership now requires a conscious *transformational* focus.

Figure 8.1 illustrates how the collective thinking about leadership has expanded over the course of the past three decades. As illustrated, each evolution incorporates the skills and awareness of the previous roles, rather than replacing them. Therefore, a competent change leader possesses the skills and competencies of a manager, leader, and change manager.

Our exploration of how the role of the leader has evolved is not intended to be a comprehensive review of the leadership theories of the past several decades. We seek only to benchmark the historic evolution of leadership. Our discussion will, therefore, be selective and brief. Also, keep in mind as we discuss each role that although any person may have the title of manager, leader, change manager, or change leader, he or she may, in fact, have the qualities and skills of any of these. It is our belief that anyone in the organization can fill any of these roles, facilitating change within his or her own sphere of influence in the organization.

Differentiation of the Roles of Manager and Leader

In the late 1970s and early 1980s, there was great debate about how to differentiate management from leadership. Many academicians, writers, and practitioners contributed to this discussion. Let's summarize.

The job of classic managers was to optimize current operations, in good Industrial Mindset fashion. Management responsibilities commonly included planning, organizing, deciding, acting, and reviewing. Managers focused on how to improve the existing business and spent most of their time identifying and solving problems that were blocking the organization's performance. When change was required, it was commonly developmental, geared toward improving what was already in place. The primary view through the manager's eyes was inside the boundaries of the organization and generally confined to short-term time frames.

While *managers* look internally to the organization, (down and in), *leaders* also look outside of the boundaries of the organization (up and out). Leaders are primarily responsible for creating clear strategic direction for the future of the organization. Leaders assume that some change will be necessary to keep up with the marketplace, so they attend to what is happening outside of the system to be able

Figure 8.1. Evolution of the Leader's Role

Change Leader
• Creates change strategy that integrates people, process, and content needs, including how to change mindset and culture to support new business directions
• Uses conscious process thinking to design the change as a fullstream process
• Models and promotes the emerging mindset and way of being to the organization
• Ensures that the change is aligned and integrated with all interdependent systems and procceses
• Catalyzes people's commitment and highest contribution to the change
• Creates and sustains conditions for success for the change, especially the continuous generation of new information
• Builds organizational capacity for ongoing change and self-renewal

Change Manager
• Manages the implementation of new directions through multiple change initiatives
• Accounts for people dynamics in change, mostly overcoming resistance
• Creates and oversees change infrastructures and resources to support the change
• Aligns the human resource systems to support business change

Leader
• Creates clear strategic direction for the future
• Looks outside of the organization's boundaries for threats and opportunities
• Communicates new requirements for performance and profit enhancement
• Motivates people to pursue new directions

Manager
• Optimizes current operations
• Focuses on how to improve the existing business
• Solves problems that are blocking performance

to forecast how the organization needs to operate to succeed in its environment. The leader then communicates the new requirements for performance and profit to the organization, and the managers carry out the new plans.

Leaders also keep a strategic eye on how well the organization is doing, set priorities, satisfy stockholder requirements, help solve strategic conflicts, and give parameters to the achievement of goals. Since the early 1980s, as the scope and pace of change began increasing, leaders have also been tasked with creating vision for their organizations. The intent of visioning is to provide clear and common direction, as well as motivation for change. While leaders always give more attention than managers to motivating and inspiring people, visioning makes the role even more distinct.

Along Comes Change Management

In the late 1980s and early 1990s, many leaders began to feel the pinch of not being successful in actually creating the visions and organizational solutions they needed to meet their increasing marketplace demands. Many of those who used big consulting firms to help them design new strategies, structures, technology, services, or products became frustrated at failing to implement the solutions they had purchased. Their frustration centered around difficulties with implementation, morale, resistance, speed of change, and resources.

The leaders who recognized this as a pattern began to ask for more from their consultants and their organizations. Determining the right change solution and announcing it to the organization was no guarantee of success, especially if the organization could not put it in place in a timely and cost-effective way. This new realization gave birth to the field of change management and the role of the change manager.

Change managers are often assumed to be lower in the organization than the leaders. Typically, they report to and serve the wishes of the leaders, which puts a limitation on their ability to influence the leaders to transform themselves as part of the organization's transformation strategy. Change managers are charged with making change happen more effectively, yet rarely attend to building leadership's capability to lead change. This may be fine for developmental or transitional change. However, this severely impairs the chances for successful transformation because the leaders' old behaviors stifle the effort.

Change managers are charged with three goals: (1) Plan how to put the change in place; (2) ensure that it actually is implemented; and (3) overcome people's resistance. To accomplish these goals, they work either with the executives or independently to translate the vision and desired outcomes into distinct change projects and then mobilize these efforts in the organization. Defining the changes as projects frequently causes them to think about these efforts as closed systems—with a beginning, middle, and end. Change managers typically employ a "project management" change model of some sort to help plan and complete the implementation.

All in all, the addition of the change manager role adds greatly to the likelihood that developmental and transitional change efforts will go better than before. However, when the organization's changes are transformational in nature, the role of the change manager is not sufficient. They are typically not prepared for the personal or organizational demands that transformation requires.

Change managers often fail to understand the various types of change and the different strategies required to lead each of them effectively. Change managers all too often assume that their change management approaches are adequate for transformation, which just isn't true. Hence the creation of the role of the change leader.

The Role of the Change Leader

As shown in Figure 8.1, the change leader possesses seven core competencies. Note that they reflect the operating principles of conscious transformation. Change leaders:

- Create change strategy that integrates people, process, and content needs, including how to change mindset and culture to support new business directions;

- Use process thinking to design and facilitate the change as a fullstream process (for example, setting the foundations for success up-front, designing the change, and implementing it);

- Model and promote the Emerging Mindset and way of being to the organization;

- Ensure that the change is aligned and integrated with all interdependent systems and processes;

- Catalyze people's commitment and highest contribution to the change;

- Create and sustain conditions for success for the change, especially the continuous generation of new information; and

- Build organizational capacity for ongoing change and self-renewal.

The amount of personal change, personal presence, skill, and awareness required increases exponentially as one proceeds from manager to leader to change manager to change leader (see Figure 8.2). The magnitude of development required for a manager to grow into a conscious change leader capable of leading transformation is astounding. The following list is just a sampling of paradigm shifts a person might have when moving from manager, viewing the world through the classical Industrial Mindset, to conscious change leader, perceiving reality with the Emerging Mindset. The person moves:

- From being responsible for a manageable, discrete function of the organization to being responsible for responding to massive uncertainties;

- From solving known problems to supporting solutions that emerge out of an unknown mix of dynamic variables;

- From installing change in the machine that is the organization to nurturing the conditions for change to emerge in a complex living system;

- From screening and hiding information about the organization's performance to sharing all information openly, even troubling or dissonant information;

- From delegating change implementation to others to fully embracing what is required to play a significant role in leading change oneself;

- From managing and controlling a single, linear change process to facilitating multiple, multi-dimensional, and interdependent change processes, all as one complex effort;

- From treating people as cost structures who work to serve the leaders' wishes to caring for people, their feelings, personal needs, and choices;

- From expecting *others* to change to engaging in *their own* personal transformation;

- From assuming they have fixed "the problem" for good to building the organization's capacity for ongoing change and self-renewal; and

- From arduously attempting to stabilize the organization to supporting chaos and disruption as healthy stepping stones to an unknown but necessary future.

Figure 8.2. Growth Required of Change Leaders

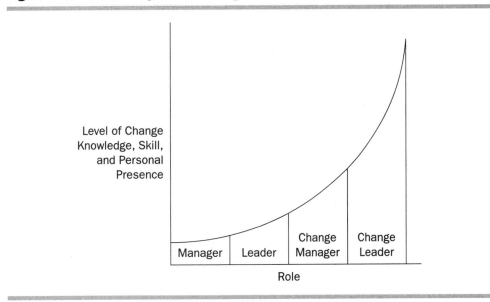

Conscious leaders embrace change as a way of life. From their point of view, they expect change and look for it. They establish the conditions, within themselves and their organizations, to respond to change as effectively and rapidly as possible. This means they will have an awareness of the subtle dynamics of transformation beyond the perceptions they held in their previous roles.

So is becoming a conscious change leader the final evolution of the role of the leader? Most definitely not. Expansion into the role of the conscious change leader is, however, the next target for executive and management development. Let's explore what it takes for people to develop into conscious change leaders.

Arenas for Development

For you to create change leaders in your organization will require a focused change leadership development strategy. Traditional development curricula focus on the expertise people need to have (knowing) and the skills or competencies they need to possess (doing). For conscious change leadership, there is a third arena of development—*being*. (See Figure 8.3.) This refers to leaders' way of being, mindset, and

Figure 8.3. Development Areas for Conscious Transformational Leaders

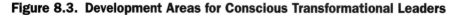

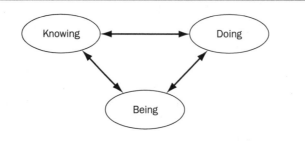

style, as discussed in Chapter Four, and brings together all of our earlier discussions of becoming more conscious—of oneself, others, and the human and process dynamics of the organization as a whole.

In this model, "knowing" refers to what conscious change leaders need to be aware of, know, and understand. Here is a partial list of topics:

- The drivers of change and that all of them are required for an accurate scope of transformation;

- That mindset is causative;

- The power and impact of perception;

- Human dynamics and motivation;

- Conscious process thinking and systems thinking;

- Culture, what it is, and how to influence it;

- The unique dynamics of transformational change and what it takes to plan for and respond to its complexity over time;

- Change strategy and the requirement for integrating content, people, and process;

- A comprehensive change process model and how to use it for transformation;

- The three leadership styles and their different treatments of process design and process facilitation; and

- The twenty-one dimensions and their interdependent nature.

The "doing" arena puts the competencies of the conscious change leader into action. Examples include:

- Building integrated change strategy;
- Defining the type of change, change imperatives, and scope;
- Creating conditions for success;
- Conscious process design and facilitation;
- Supporting people through their emotional transitions;
- Drawing out people's diverse views and facilitating agreement and alignment for the overall good of the change and the organization;
- Building and communicating the case for change;
- Crafting and establishing a shared vision; and
- Engaging the whole organization in shaping the change, learning from the process, and working together to fulfill the vision.

The "being" arena is where traditional executive development becomes interesting. Being is the foundation of transformation and, therefore, is central to the development of conscious transformational change leaders. We defined "way of being" in Chapter Four as the aggregate expression of one's mindset, emotions, and behavior. Remember that *mindset* includes fundamental assumptions, core beliefs, attitudes, and values. *Behavior* includes leadership style and personality characteristics. As an integrated whole, they become a person's way of being. They shape how one expresses himself or herself and how one impacts others (which, by the way, is equally a function of *their* way of being).

The benefits of becoming conscious of your way of being include:

- Modeling the organization's transformation while leading it, which adds enormous credibility to the effort;
- Being authentic—your natural self—rather than trying to act in some artificial or externally mandated fashion;
- Being fully present no matter what is going on; being skilled in self-mastery;
- Getting to the truth of any situation faster;
- Understanding your part in creating results (both good results and bad);

- Making better decisions;

- Appreciating what is happening in any given situation and why, in order to accept it for what it is and how to change it;

- Being able to unravel your perception of reality from the facts of reality; and

- Developing your intuition and being able to sense right action and right timing.

The "being" component, when fully engaged, is witnessed in people who are clear about what they are committed to and why; express their emotions without damaging others; and align what they *know* with what they *do* in effective ways. People who attend to their internal dynamics of being tend to be better listeners and have the ability to be fully "present" with others. They can more readily access their intuition, out-of-the-box thinking, and their proven expertise—and bring all of this to bear on a situation.

We emphasize the being arena because of the critical skills and insights it unleashes for successful transformation. However, because it is new for many leaders, the being arena can carry both excitement and fear. Clearly, most leaders are more comfortable with the knowledge and action buckets, not only in leading transformation, but in the other aspects of their personal and professional lives as well. *Knowing* and *doing* are more controllable, familiar, and measurable. Consequently, supporting leaders to attend to "being" should be done by skilled facilitators. In our own leadership breakthrough programs, we consistently see leaders' fear about being quickly turn into excitement as they discover the profound positive impact being has on their experience and results. There is definitely an art in teaching being.

It is important to note that the concept of "way of being" is defined differently in various cultures around the world. Some languages do not have a word that translates into what we mean by "way of being." You may need to work with the notion and translate it as closely as possible for the benefit of people with diverse backgrounds. Everyone has ways of being. As a descriptor of internal reality, it just may need to be tailored to fit cultural norms and orientations. Words such as leadership style, ways of relating to others, attitude, human reactions, emotional expression, and behavior may be helpful.

As we have emphasized, for the majority of people, personal growth and change are necessary before one can come fully into his or her role as a change leader. However, promoting personal change has often been the greatest challenge (and risk) for executive development directors. Fast-track companies, as well as the more traditional utility, engineering, and manufacturing organizations, have historically had little tolerance or openness to the personal or being arena. Sadly, we still hear remarks from HR development specialists such as, "We are forbidden to name or address anything personal or humanistic here. We are forced to teach only information and skills. Nothing touchy-feely!" In these companies, we usually find managers trying desperately to lead, but failing, and change managers struggling in their transformation efforts. Unless these organizations wake up and recognize the limiting consequences of their mindset about the being arena, the evolution from manager to change leader will be many years away for them.

The human resource and training industry's approach to personal growth training has historically contributed to these organizations' skepticisms. Many personal growth trainings are, in fact, too "touchy-feely" and void of any direct connection to increasing real-world results. Personal change trainings offered in organizations must be: (1) results-based, (2) founded on pragmatic approaches, (3) applicable on the job, (4) made credible by rational reasons for how personal change can contribute to performance and well-being, and (5) emotionally safe.[1]

The being arena is the very path that is required for traditional organizations' continued success. We believe that, like vision and empowerment before it, being and deep personal change, when taught properly, will become recognized and pursued as essential for organizations to thrive and sustain themselves over time. The time is now.

A Curriculum for Developing Conscious Change Leaders

We believe that all organizations should be seeking to develop their own internal capacity to transform. Certainly, many core business functions can be outsourced, but transformation should not be one of them. Transformation will only become more of a necessity in the future, not less.

Relying on outside firms to "transform" your company is not a path to success, in our opinion. Certainly, outside guidance and expertise have an essential place and should be used. Thought leaders bring value, and external consultants may

---

[1]You may contact our organization, Being First, for a free article entitled "Making Personal Change Training Work in Organizations."

possess expertise that your organization lacks. However, outsiders should be fit into *your* transformation efforts, not the other way around.

This requires partnership, yet your leaders and employees must possess the foundational capacity to be full players in the partnership. Otherwise, it is too easy to default to the external contractors. Therefore, whether you are serious about developing your own internal expertise to guide transformation or want to use mostly outside vendors, we believe you still must develop baseline change leadership competencies.

We believe that all organizations need a change leadership development curriculum to supplement their existing executive, management, supervisory, and employee development curricula. How robust your change leadership curriculum is will depend on your desired outcomes. The following discussion is oriented toward leaders and consultants who are choosing to develop thorough change capability at the *executive and management levels.*

Many variables influence the design of a change leadership curriculum, such as current marketplace trends, current level of executive and management capability, existence of internal OD consultants and their capacity, budget, structure of the organization, established cultural norms regarding coaching and learning, and so forth. We offer a generic curriculum below as food for thought. You will undoubtedly need to tailor it to fit your needs.

Design Principles

The ten operating principles of conscious transformation offer tremendous insight into the requirements for building a change leadership development curriculum. The two principles that stand out as critical are "multi-dimensional" and "continuous process over time." Why? Too often we encounter executive and management development curricula that are one-dimensional and/or based on a single yearly training event. They often focus on externally based skills, such as finance, marketing, and business development, and neglect internal dimensions, such as mindset, emotions, and relationships. Even though external skills can be taught in singular events better than internal dynamics can, a process approach would benefit both areas.

Developing transformational change skills requires leaders and consultants to learn throughout the full lifecycle of their organization's transformation process. For example, change leaders cannot learn about implementation in the classroom and then expect to apply their learning effectively eighteen months later in their change effort. Change leadership development curricula should be based on at least a one-year time frame, if not two or three.

Change leadership development must blend classroom learning with field application. All change leadership development should be "case based." There is no reason to remain purely theoretical or conceptual. All change leaders should enter the curriculum with a live change effort to work on. If they do not have one, then they should either partner with someone who does or wait until a later date to join the program.

We believe that change leadership development should integrate leaders, consultants, and other change agents into the same programs and processes where possible. They should not automatically be kept separate. As we have said, leaders and consultants must partner for successful transformation. Throughout the book we have referred to both as "change leaders," usually not differentiating between the two. The required partnership cannot occur if the groups are always kept in different rooms. Having said this, there are definite times when they should learn in separate forums. We will make those times clear as we discuss the five components of change leadership development.

Framework for a Change Leadership Development Curriculum

Change leadership development requires five distinct but interconnected areas of activity. You will need to translate this framework into a *process*. Otherwise, you might inadvertently think you can simply offer separate courses in each area and have an effective curriculum. Please don't make this common mistake.

The elements of the framework follow:

- Breakthrough Training
- Change Education
- Building Change Strategy
- Conscious Process Design
- Conscious Process Facilitation

Breakthrough Training. This element of the framework is primarily focused on shifting change leaders' mindsets from an industrial worldview to the Emerging Mindset. This work must be experiential. Didactic approaches don't work because breakthrough training is not meant to teach leaders *about* the Emerging Mindset; it must help them *adopt* the Emerging Mindset. Keeping a process perspective, however, it is important to realize that no training event is going to replace anyone's conditioned mindset overnight. This work is a lifelong process, and the curriculum must support this development over time. However, breakthrough training must have enough emotional and experiential impact to open the doors of people's awareness to the reality of the Emerging Mindset.

In our experience, the most effective way to do this is to ensure that the design of the breakthrough programs integrates as many of the twenty-one dimensions as possible. In our programs, we experientially attend to the levels of self, relationship, team, and organization. We also deal experientially with physical, emotional, mental, and spiritual domains in all of the levels. This provides one integrated experience of the Emerging Mindset perspective, making this worldview both more tangible and more plausible.

Breakthrough training must be behavior- and results-oriented, as well as focused on underlying assumptions and beliefs. Peoples' internal experience must be translated into how they are actually going to lead transformation differently to achieve greater results. The program must directly deal with self-limiting behaviors and emotions, as well as the participants' desired ways of being. A number of behavioral topics we focus on in our breakthrough programs include behavioral styles analysis, team dynamics, communication skills (listening and speaking), dialogue, interpersonal dynamics, team visioning, personal power, interfacing with conflict, self-management, and personal transformation. Remember that any attention to behavioral change must also address the underlying mindsets and assumptions that have generated the old behaviors and that will create the insight and opportunity for new behavior. Otherwise, your program won't produce real personal change—only minor or temporary behavioral change.[2]

Change Education. This element of the framework provides leaders with an overview of the information and models that they need to understand to lead their transformations effectively. Education, by its very nature, is geared at *understanding*, not at mindset or behavioral change, although it may catalyze also. Change education formats include classroom presentations, case studies and discussion/

---

[2]Please refer to the "being" components in the Appendix for an additional list of topics we have found essential to address experientially in breakthrough programs.

learning groups, reading, and application tools. Most of these change education topics are covered in *The Change Leader's Roadmap,* the companion volume to this book. The Appendix lists knowledge areas that might be considered for this element of your curriculum. The list also includes areas that are essential to change leaders' development, even though many of them might be supported through other programs or in different ways.

Building Change Strategy. This element of the framework focuses on real-time change strategy development, including how to address the *content* and *people* elements of the organization's transformations using a *process* approach. Exhibit 8.1 shows a template for building a change strategy. It references a series of inputs that are developed in Phase I of the Change Process Model, as well as the elements of the change strategy itself. This component must be done on live change efforts by teams of change leaders and their change consultants. The output of this component is both learning and a real change strategy.

Exhibit 8.1. Template for Building a Change Strategy

Inputs from Phase I

- ☐ Case for change, including:
    - ☐ Drivers of change;
    - ☐ Initial desired outcomes for the transformation;
    - ☐ Leverage points for transformation;
    - ☐ Type of change;
    - ☐ Scope of the change;
    - ☐ Targets of the change; and
    - ☐ Degree of urgency;
- ☐ Project community;
- ☐ Organizational readiness assessment results;
- ☐ Leadership capacity assessment; and
- ☐ Conditions for success.

Exhibit 8.1. Template for Building a Change Strategy, Cont'd

Elements of Change Strategy

☐ How to unify all initiatives under one transformational umbrella;

☐ Position of this transformation in the organization;

☐ Bold actions;

☐ Strategic levers;

☐ Participation strategies for creating a critical mass of commitment;

☐ Change infrastructure;

☐ Milestone events from Phases I through IX; and

☐ General timeline.

Conscious Process Design. This element of the framework is also handled on live change efforts by teams of change leaders and their consultants. It consists of tailoring the nine-phase Change Process Model to support the real work they believe will be required in their organization's complete transformation, taking into account the twenty-one dimensions. Ideally change leaders must do this process design with a facilitative style in mind. If that is not their natural style, then coaching can be very useful to help them develop that style while they engage in the strategic work of process design. In this case, the output will be both a more refined change process and change leadership development.

Conscious Process Facilitation. This element of the framework is learned as the real-time action of the transformation plays out. It is usually supported with learning clinics, coaching, and just-in-time consultation between change leaders and their consultants. It further reinforces learning and course correction, process design, and any personal development work that is required to support the leaders as they move through the full lifecycle of their organization's transformations.

Summary

In this chapter, we focused on what is required to develop conscious change leaders. We addressed how the role of the leader has evolved from being a manager, to leader, to change manager, to change leader. We explored the arenas for developing change leaders—knowing, doing, and being—and offered a template for designing a transformational change leader development curriculum. This was provided as food for thought as you consider the needs of your organization and how much of this competency you choose to build into it.

The next chapter brings our exploration of conscious transformation to a close. We have offered much for you to think about and consider, as both a change leader and a consultant. The chapter offers a series of focused questions to help you attend to the choices you have to make about your own transformation as a change leader.

The Leadership Choice to Transform

THERE IS NO FORMULA THAT GUARANTEES successful organizational transformation. There is no absolute right or wrong way to lead change. It has merely been our intention to expand your understanding and options for consciously leading your organization into the future. Whether you are a consultant or an organizational leader, you have choices to make about how you will proceed to advance your change leadership capacity.

Our desire has been to make this book immediately useful to you. We offer some important questions to consider as you reflect on what you have read and how to put it into action in your work. They will assist you to make conscious and committed choices for expanding your change leadership impact in positive ways. We entertain these questions regularly. They keep us alert, growing, and responsible. Consider them for yourself.

1. Is your current style and approach to transformation producing the results you want?

Conscious transformation begins with the choice to achieve something different from what currently exists. If you are completely satisfied with the results you are achieving as a change leader or consultant, congratulations! If not, what, specifically, is not going the way you would like? To what do you attribute the gap between what you are achieving and what you choose to produce? What do you need to do more of or less of?

2. Are you attracted to what we have described as conscious transformational change leadership? In what ways and why?

If you were excited or moved by our discussions about transformational change, mindset, conscious process thinking, the Emerging Mindset, or any other topic, focus on what was so compelling to you. Why are these topics important to what you are dealing with or where you are in your development, job, or practice? What has stuck with you, mentally and emotionally? How can these particular concepts or tools add value to you and your pursuits as a change leader?

3. What are your intentions for your future work? Why do you want to do what you are setting out to do?

Sometimes people are attracted to something and don't understand why. The pursuit of what is compelling to you can be fueled by becoming clear about what you want to create and what is motivating you. Knowing the desired outcome of your efforts makes choice points along the way much easier. What is the reward or benefit you seek from your work?

4. What impact do you want to have on others as you work?

Beyond knowing what you want to produce in tangible terms, it is helpful to also understand how you want to be perceived and received by others whom you impact along the way. Some leaders have identified wanting to be seen as visionary, smart, compassionate, supportive, competent, charismatic, or powerful. Consultants frequently report wanting to be seen as insightful, perceptive, competent, balanced, or helpful. How do you want to be in your role, and what perception would you want to produce in the people whose lives you influence? Knowing this will help you consciously shape your approach and behavior.

5. What strengths do you have that you want to build on as you create your new way of working and leading?

Your strengths have gotten you to where you are. Even if you are considering a significant transformation in your way of working, you will want to identify the things that you are good at or that give you the most pleasure or satisfaction. Should things become difficult as you go through your development process, you can always rely on your strengths as you work on developing your weaknesses.

6. If working with or influencing others is required in your job or life, how will you engage others in creating shared clarity and intention for the outcome you collectively choose?

It is one thing to get yourself on board with your own action plan for change; it is another to create a shared intention for change with others. As you have clarified your own choices, you can support others to do the same. How will you facilitate the process of going through this development together? What is required to achieve group alignment and then sustain it? How will you establish and sustain shared responsibility for this among everyone involved?

7. How will you build your own or others' capacity for change?

You and others may need to develop your capacity for change, relying on new knowledge, skill, behavior, or ways of being and relating that are different from what currently exists. How will you do this for yourself? How will you facilitate this for others?

You might create learning groups to support each other's process and share fears, insights, breakthroughs, and best practices. You might create a way to teach each other about what you are learning or considering. This is a powerful strategy for keeping the energy for your development vital. Another strategy is to ensure cross-training among different types of people who have diverse expertise. Create mentor relationships. Set up a communications network designed for participants to share across organizational boundaries, or matrix people in project teams on live change initiatives with the intent to share knowledge and skills, as well as support one another's shifts in their ways of being.

8. What personal belief, emotion, or behavior patterns stand in the way of your development? What will you do to alter them?

A significant and challenging part of changing mindset is uncovering the deep-rooted negative thought patterns and beliefs that inadvertently sabotage people's good intentions to change and grow. Without bringing these inhibitors to the surface, they will continue to compete for your energy and attention, thereby weighing you down or sinking your efforts altogether. Once you identify these emotions and beliefs, they will not necessarily disappear, but you can learn to react to them with more awareness, better understanding, and the intention not to energize or follow them.

We have helped leaders and consultants identify such self-limiting beliefs as "I'll never succeed," "I'm not capable," or "If I fail, I'll look like a fool, and people will laugh or scorn me." They have surfaced patterns such as "If a woman tells me what to do, she must be wrong," "If I'm not the first to act, I'll be a loser," and "Do whatever it takes to look good and be right." Recognizing the destructive behaviors that follow these beliefs is not difficult! Uncovering that they exist and are blocking your path to more conscious leadership is essential to getting them out of your way.

9. What other conditions or circumstances do you see blocking your ability to proceed as you wish?

Some people perceive reasons outside of their own influence as the cause of their lack of growth or action. It is actually quite easy to project the cause of one's failure on the external world. We have heard people blame their current work environment, their spouses, their financial obligations, or their bosses or parents for their inability to make a change. The range of targets is endless. Again, it is essential to identify these forces as players in your reality, note their part, and minimize or overcome their control over your destiny.

10. What actions will you take to get started or make the changes you are choosing?

If you could choose three areas of development for yourself and for your organization, what would they be? What actions do you need to take to get started? Perhaps choose one knowledge area, one skill, and one "way of being" or personal quality that speaks the loudest to you. Of course, you can do more, and we suggest that you begin with identifying three achievable action steps that will leverage your development as a conscious change leader.

Summary

Perhaps the most critical success factor in choosing to become a conscious transformational change leader is to take a personal stand for yourself and your action plan. All kinds of distractions and obstacles will likely surface, yet your choice to proceed, to support yourself to continue, is the critical requirement for progress. If you are partnering with others, you can coach one another to keep yourselves fully committed despite challenges. You will undoubtedly need to balance your day-to-day responsibilities with your personal change plans, as the two will happen concurrently. This is all a part of engaging consciously and intentionally in your own transformation.

We have asked you to consider many questions about your choice to move in the direction of greater consciousness in your leadership and consulting. For us, there really isn't a question about *whether*; it is all about *how.* The complexities of the 21st Century global business environment demand change toward greater awareness in order to transform organizations to meet the human, marketplace, and environmental needs of the times. Collectively, leaders and consultants must continually make decisions that balance the needs of people, the organization, and society at large. Leaders must create business strategies that add to their organizations' future viability *and* the well-being of people and communities.

The message of the Emerging Mindset is clear. Leaders and consultants must hear this message because they carry so much positional power to influence and transform social and organizational systems. Granted, fully embracing and carrying out this message requires tremendous courage and personal change. However, we believe wholeheartedly that today's leaders and consultants have the ability.

Certainly, the personal transformation required is the greatest challenge of all and demands the deepest commitment. The inner journey of softening the rigidity of the Industrial Mindset's conditioning is a lifelong process for all of us. Expanding our awareness and opening our hearts and minds to new ways of being takes diligent daily attention. And the most subtle challenge, the one that delivers the greatest of rewards, is reducing the role of autopilot to its rightful place and nurturing our ability to witness our world—consciously. This process of waking ourselves up to more of what is possible is our direct path to leading transformation successfully.

However, our challenge does not stop here. Deciding to develop ourselves in the direction we propose is within our own personal control and desires. The next challenge that awaits us is in how to generate the wake-up call for all of the leaders and consultants who do not yet seem to recognize or care about the long-term implications of today's organizational decisions or the short-term trauma and risk they impose on employees. The challenge is in getting the attention of a critical mass of these leaders and consultants to raise their conscious awareness of new ways of being and leading. The challenge is in making the conscious approach attractive to them so that they, too, will turn inward and expand their conscious awareness and fully unleash the possibilities of our collective future.

It is our hope that this book, coupled with the world's growing awareness of the need for personal, organizational, social, and global transformation, will help both to sound the alarm and to mobilize the inspiration and choice to lead transformation consciously.

Appendix:
Development Arenas for Conscious Change Leaders

This Appendix provides three lists of topics to consider when designing a curriculum to develop conscious change leaders. The three are the *knowledge* arena (information, models, ways of thinking); the *doing* arena (skills, abilities, and actions); and the *being* arena (styles, mindset, and traits). The lists are extensive; do not assume that your curriculum needs to include all of them. Select what fits your needs and tailor appropriately. Keep in mind that much of what is listed reflects the material in this book and in *The Change Leader's Roadmap*.

You can customize and use these checklists as assessment tools as well. To do so, determine the information you want to generate from the lists (for example, do you want to know whether you have *mastered* an item, have *adequate competency* in it, or *need to develop* in it). Based on the answer, read each list and identify the items that you have mastered by putting an "M" on the line in front of them; those in which you have adequate competency with an "A"; and those that need development with a "D." You do not have to assess your competency in any item that is not relevant to your situation. If you need further understanding of an item, refer back to the text of either book.

Knowledge Arena

___ Three types of change (developmental, transitional, and transformational);

___ The differences between the Industrial Mindset and the Emerging Mindset;

___ Conscious process thinking, design, and facilitation;

___ Nine-phase Change Process Model for Leading Conscious Transformation;

___ Change strategy and its components of content, people, and process;

___ Drivers of Change Model; how to define and establish imperatives for change;

___ Mindset and how to change it; understanding that "mindset is causative"; the dynamics of perception;

___ Human dynamics and motivation;

___ Change capacity and readiness and how to build them;

___ Participation strategies and how to engage the whole organization in the change;

___ How people respond to change and how to support them through their transition cycle;

___ Temporary change support structures, systems, and policies;

___ Organizational culture and how to change it;

___ What it takes to build and sustain good working relationships and teams;

___ How to generate collaboration and efficiencies across change initiatives;

___ Levels of design and how to apply them;

___ Five levels of communication;

___ Elements of organization; organization design model;

___ Learning and course correcting;

___ The process of personal transformation; and

___ Strategies of changing organizational mindset.

Doing Arena

___ Using conscious process design and facilitation skills;

___ Defining imperatives for change (for example, business, organizational, cultural);

___ Determining the type and scope of the change;

___ Defining and staffing change leadership roles;

___ Determining the leaders' and organization's level of readiness and capacity for making the change;

___ Developing an integrated change strategy;

___ Tailoring and applying the nine-phase Change Process Model;

___ Identifying the prevailing mindset, determining the required mindset, and changing mindset individually and collectively;

___ Ensuring that the decision-making process is overt;

___ Using coaching and counseling skills for assisting people through each stage in their cycle of emotions;

___ Creating diverse teams, drawing out diverse views, and facilitating alignment for the greater good;

___ Using multi-directional communication skills;

___ Determining, establishing, and monitoring conditions for success;

___ Creating shared vision;

___ Consciously choosing who is best to participate in change activities;

___ Proactively course correcting for the change process;

___ Generating information and using it effectively to support the transformation; thinking "outside the box";

___ Partnering with others to support the shared vision—dialogue;

___ Dealing effectively with politics;

___ Practicing self-mastery and personal development;

___ Engaging the whole organization in shaping the change;

___ Learning as an individual, team, or organization;

___ Coaching; counseling with compassion;

___ Seeking, giving, and receiving feedback;

___ Resolving conflict and building alignment;

___ Recognizing wake-up calls for course correction;

___ Managing resources creatively to support the change;

___ Mobilizing and sustaining a critical mass of support for the change; and

___ Identifying the impacts of any event or plan on the change process, people, the culture or the organization, and all other interdependent systems and processes.

Being Arena

___ Valuing self-awareness;

___ Being personally responsible;

___ Telling the truth;

___ Understanding and caring about people's needs and desires;

___ Being supportive;

___ Having personal integrity;

___ Being committed to the shared vision;

___ Doing what is right for the good of the whole system;

___ Being authentic; dealing effectively with your own emotions;

___ Staying in relationship during conflict or difference;

___ Honoring people's diverse contributions and needs;

___ Being willing to self-reflect and change personally;

___ Being able to take a stand and be courageous;

___ Being able to tolerate uncertainty and prolonged ambiguity;

___ Having a sense of discovery, being "in the inquiry" about how the change is going;

___ Being balanced between knowing, doing, and being; balanced between organizational and human issues; balanced among body, emotions, mind, and spirit;

___ Being vulnerable and taking responsibility for mistakes;

___ Honoring and accepting differences and diversity;

___ Empowering others; creating conditions for others to contribute their best;

___ Being flexible and adaptable;

___ Being willing to communicate with others about your internal state, concerns, reactions, mental models;

___ Being positive, optimistic, and intentional about what you want to create;

___ Taking risks;

___ Walking the talk of your values and principles; and

___ Seeking out creative solutions.

Bibliography

Ackerman Anderson, L. (1986). Development, transition or transformation: The question of change in organizations. *OD Practitioner, 18*(4).

Ackerman Anderson, L., & Anderson, D. (1996). *Facilitating large systems change participant manual.* Durango, CO: Being First, Inc.

Ackerman Anderson, L., & Anderson, D. (2001). *The change leader's roadmap: How to navigate your organization's transformation.* San Francisco: Jossey-Bass/Pfeiffer.

Adams, J. (1984). *Transforming work: A collection of organizational transformation readings.* Alexandria, VA: Miles River Press.

Adams, J. (1986). *Transforming leadership: From vision to results.* Alexandria, VA: Miles River Press.

Anderson, D. (1986). *Optimal performance manual.* Durango, CO: Being First, Inc.

Alban, B., & Bunker, B. (1997). *Large group interventions: Engaging the whole system for rapid change.* San Francisco: Jossey-Bass.

Argyris, C. (1985). *Strategy, change, and defensive routines.* Marshfield, MA: Pitman.

Ashkenas, R., Ulrich, R., Jick, T., & Kerr, S. (1995). *The boundaryless organization: Breaking the chains of organizational structure.* San Francisco: Jossey-Bass.

Axelrod, R. (1992). *Terms of engagement: Changing the way we change our organizations.* San Francisco: Berrett-Koehler.

Beck, D., & Cohen, C. (1996). *Spiral dynamics: Mastering values, leadership, and change.* Cambridge, MA: Blackwell.

Beckhard, R. (1997). *Agent of change: My life, my practice.* San Francisco: Jossey-Bass.

Beckhard, R., & Harris, R. (1987). *Organizational transitions.* Reading, MA: Addison-Wesley.

Bennis, W. (1989). *Why leaders can't lead: The unconscious conspiracy continues.* San Francisco: Jossey-Bass.

Bennis, W. (1995). *On becoming a leader* (audio). New York: Simon & Schuster.

Bennis, W., & Nanus, B. (1985). *Leaders: The strategies for taking charge.* New York: Harper & Row.

Blanchard, K., & Hersey, P. (1982). *Management of organizational behavior: Utilizing human resources.* Upper Saddle River, NJ: Prentice Hall.

Blanchard, K., & O'Connor, M. (1997). *Managing by values.* San Francisco: Berrett-Koehler.

Block, P. (1999). *Flawless consulting: A guide to getting your expertise used* (2nd ed.). San Francisco: Jossey-Bass/Pfeiffer.

Bohm, D. (1980). *Wholeness and the implicate order.* New York: Routledge.

Bridges, W. (1980). *Transitions* (2nd ed.). New York: Perseus Publishing.

Bridges, W. (1991). *Managing transitions: Making the most of change.* Reading, MA: Addison-Wesley.

Bridges, W. (1994). *Jobshift: How to prosper in a workplace without jobs.* Reading, MA: Addison-Wesley.

Briggs, J., & Peat, D. (1989). *Turbulent mirror: An illustrated guide to chaos theory and the science of wholeness.* New York: Harper & Row.

Briggs, J., & Peat, F.D. (1999). *Seven life lessons of chaos: Spiritual wisdom from the science of change.* New York: HarperCollins.

Bunker, B., & Alban, B. (Eds.). (1992/December). Large group interventions. [Special issue] *Applied Behavioral Science, (28)*4.

Capra, F. (1983). *The turning point: Science, society, and the rising culture.* New York: Bantam.

Capra, F. (1991). *The tao of physics: An exploration of the parallels between modern physics and eastern mysticism.* Boston, MA: Shambhala.

Capra, F. (1996). *The web of life.* New York: Anchor Press.

Case, J. (1998). *The open-book experience: Lessons from over 100 companies who successfully transformed themselves.* Reading, MA: Addison-Wesley.

Collins, J., & Porras, J. (1994). *Built to last: Successful habits of visionary companies.* New York: HarperCollins.

Conger, J., Spreitzer, G., & Lawler, E., III (1999). *The leader's change handbook: An essential guide to setting direction and taking action.* San Francisco: Jossey-Bass.

Conner, D. (1993). *Managing at the speed of change: How resilient managers succeed and prosper where others fail.* New York: Villard Books.

Conner, D. (1998). *Leading at the edge of chaos: How to create the nimble organization.* New York: John Wiley & Sons.

Csikszentmihalyi, M. (1990). *Flow: The psychology of optimal experience.* New York: Harper & Row.

De Chardin, P. (1962). *Human energy.* New York: Harcourt Brace Jovanovich.

Deal, T., & Kennedy, A. (1982). *Corporate cultures: The rites and rituals of corporate life.* Reading, MA: Addison-Wesley.

Drucker, P. (1999). *Management challenges for the 21st century.* New York: HarperCollins.

Dym, B. (1995). *Readiness and change in couple therapy.* New York: HarperCollins.

Ferguson, M., & Naisbitt, J. (1980). *The aquarian conspiracy.* Los Angeles: Jeremy P. Tarcher.

Forrester, J. (1961). *Industrial dynamics.* Cambridge, MA: MIT Press.

Francis, D., & Woodcock, M. (1990). *Unblocking organizational values.* Glenview, IL: Scott, Foresman.

Frenier, C. (1997). *Business and the feminine principle: The untapped resource.* Boston, MA: Butterworth-Heinemann.

Galbraith, J., Lawler, E., & Associates. (1993). *Organizing for the future: The new logic for managing complex organizations.* San Francisco: Jossey-Bass.

Gleick, J. (1987). *Chaos: Making a new science.* New York: Penguin.

Gleick, J. (1999). *Faster: The acceleration of just about everything.* New York: Pantheon.

Goldstein, J. (1994). *The unshackled organization: Facing the challenge of unpredictability through spontaneous reorganization.* Portland, OR: Productivity Press.

Goleman, D. (1995). *Emotional intelligence: Why it can matter more than IQ.* New York: Bantam.

Greenleaf, R. (1977). *Servant leadership: A journey into the nature of legitimate power and greatness.* Mahwah, NJ: Paulist Press.

Grof, S. (1993). *The holotropic mind: The three levels of human consciousness and how they shape our lives.* New York: HarperCollins.

Gross, T. (1996). *The last word on power: Executive re-invention for leaders who must make the impossible happen.* New York: Doubleday.

Hagberg, J. (1984). *Real power: Stages of personal power in organizations.* Minneapolis, MN: Winston Press.

Hall, B. (1995). *Values shift: A guide to personal & organizational transformation.* Rockport, MA: Twin Lights Publishers.

Hammer, M., & Champy, J. (1993). *Reengineering the corporation: A manifesto for business revolution.* New York: HarperCollins.

Hammond, S. (1996). *The thin book of appreciative inquiry* (2nd ed.). Plano, TX: Thin Book Publishing.

Hammond, S., & Royal, C. (1998). *Lessons from the field: Applying appreciative inquiry.* Plano, TX: Practical Press.

Heisenberg, W. (1958). *Physics and philosophy.* New York: Harper Torchbooks.

Henricks, G., & Ludeman, K. (1996). *The corporate mystic: A guidebook for visionaries with their feet on the ground.* New York: Bantam.

Herbert, N. (1985). *Quantum reality: Beyond the new physics.* New York: Doubleday.

Herman, S. (1994). *The tao at work: On leading and following.* San Francisco: Jossey-Bass.

Hesselbein, F., Goldsmith, M., & Beckhard, R. (1996). *The leader of the future: New visions, strategies, and practices for the next era.* San Francisco: Jossey-Bass.

Huxley, A. (1956). *The doors of perception and heaven and hell.* New York: Harper Colophon.

Jacobs, R. (1994). *Real time strategic change: How to involve an entire organization in fast and far-reaching change.* San Francisco: Berrett-Koehler.

James, W. (1999). *The varieties of religious experience: A study in human nature.* New York: The Modern Library.

Jantsch, E. (1980). *The self-organizing universe.* New York: Pergamon Press.

Jaynes, J. (1990). *The origin of consciousness in the breakdown of the bicameral mind.* Boston, MA: Houghton Mifflin.

Johnson, B. (1996). *Polarity management: Identifying and managing unsolvable problems.* Amherst, MA: HRD Press.

Jones, J., & Bearley, W. (1996). *360-degree feedback: Strategies, tactics, and techniques for developing leaders.* Amherst, MA: HRD Press.

Jung, C. (1963). *Memories, dreams, reflections.* New York: Random House.

Jung, C. (1973). *Synchronicity: An acausal connecting principle.* Princeton, NJ: Princeton University Press.

Kanter, R. (1983). *The change masters: Innovation for productivity in the American corporation.* New York: Simon & Schuster.

Katzenbach, J., & Smith, D. (1993). *The wisdom of teams: Creating the high performance organization.* Boston, MA: Harvard Business School Press.

Klein, E., & Izzo, J. (1998). *Awakening corporate soul: Four paths to unleash the power of people at work.* Lions Bay, British Columbia, Canada: Fairwinds Press.

Koestenbaum, P. (1991). *Leadership: The inner side of greatness.* San Francisco: Jossey-Bass.

Kotter, J. (1996). *Leading change.* Boston, MA: Harvard Business School Press.

Kouzes, J., & Posner, B. (1995). *The leadership challenge: How to keep getting extraordinary things done in organizations.* San Francisco: Jossey-Bass.

Kouzes, J., & Posner, B. (1999). *Encouraging the heart: A leader's guide to rewarding and recognizing others.* San Francisco: Jossey-Bass.

Kuhn, T. (1962). *The structure of scientific revolutions* (1st ed.). Chicago, IL: The University of Chicago Press.

Land, G., & Jarman, B. (1992). *Breakpoint and beyond: Mastering the future today.* San Francisco: HarperCollins.

Laszlo, E., Grof, S., & Russell, P. (1999). *The consciousness revolution.* Boston, MA: Element Books.

Lebow, R., & Simon, W. (1997). *Lasting change: The shared values process that makes companies great.* New York: John Wiley & Sons.

Liebau, P. (1985). *Thoughts on relationships.* London, Ontario, Canada: P.S.A. Ventures.

Lipnack, J., & Stamps, J. (1993). *The teamnet factor: Bringing the power of boundary crossing into the heart of your business.* Essex Junction, VT: Oliver Wright.

London, M. (1988). *Change agents: New roles and innovation strategies for human resource professionals.* San Francisco: Jossey-Bass.

Lovelock, J.E. (1987). *Gaia.* London, England: Oxford University Press.

Maslow, A. (1964). *Religions, values, and peak experiences.* New York: Penguin.

Maslow, A. (1999). *Toward a psychology of being* (3rd ed.). New York: John Wiley & Sons.

Maynard, H., & Mehrtens, S. (1993). *The fourth wave: Business in the 21st century.* San Francisco: Berrett-Koehler.

McFarland, L., Senn, L., & Childress, J. (1994). *21st century leadership: Dialogues with 100 top leaders.* Los Angeles: The Leadership Press.

Miles, R. (1997). *Leading corporate transformation: A blueprint for business renewal.* San Francisco: Jossey-Bass.

Mink, O., Mink, B., Downes, E., & Owen, K. (1994). *Open organizations: A model for effectiveness, renewal, and intelligent change.* San Francisco: Jossey-Bass.

Morton, C. (1984). *Managing operations in emerging companies.* Reading, MA: Addison-Wesley.

Nadler, D. (1998). *Champions of change: How CEO's and their companies are mastering the skills of radical change.* San Francisco: Jossey-Bass.

Nadler, D, Shaw, R., & Walton, A. (1995). *Discontinuous change: Leading organizational transformation.* San Francisco: Jossey-Bass.

Nadler, D., & Tushman, M.L. (1977). A diagnostic model for organizational behavior. In J.R. Hackman, E.E. Lawler, & L.W. Porter (Eds.), *Perspectives on behavior in organizations.* New York: McGraw-Hill.

Naisbitt, J., & Aburdene, P. (1985). *Re-inventing the corporation: Transforming your job and your company for the new information society.* New York: Warner Books.

Nevis, E., Lancourt, J., & Vassallo, H. (1996). *Intentional revolutions: A seven-point strategy for transforming organizations.* San Francisco: Jossey-Bass.

Oshry, B. (1992). *The possibilities of organization.* Boston, MA: Power & Systems.

Oshry, B. (1995). *Seeing systems: Unlocking the mysteries of organizational life.* San Francisco: Berrett-Koehler.

Pascarella, P., & Frohman, M. (1989). *The purpose-driven organization: Unleashing the power of direction and commitment.* San Francisco: Jossey-Bass.

Peat, D. (1987). *Synchronicity: The bridge between matter and mind.* New York: Bantam.

Penfield, W. (1975). *Mystery of the mind: A critical study of consciousness.* Princeton, NJ: Princeton University Press.

Peters, T., & Waterman, R.H. (1982). *In search of excellence.* New York: Harper & Row.

Pribram, K. (1971). *Languages of the brain: Experimental paradoxes and principles in neuropsychology.* New York: Brandon House.

The Price Waterhouse Change Integration Team. (1995). *Better change: Best practices for transforming your organization.* New York: Irwin.

Prigogine, I. (1997). *The end of certainty: Time, chaos, and the new laws of nature.* New York: The Free Press.

Prigogine, I., & Stenger, I. (1984). *Order out of chaos.* New York: Bantam.

Ralston, F. (1995). *Hidden dynamics: How emotions affect business performance & how you can harness their power for positive results.* New York: American Management Association.

Ray, M., & Rinzler, A. (1993). *The new paradigm in business: Emerging strategies for leadership and organizational change.* New York: Tarcher/Pergee.

Reder, A. (1995). *75 best business practices for socially responsible companies.* New York: Tarcher/Putnam.

Renesch, J. (Ed.). (1992). *New traditions in business: Spirit and leadership in the 21st century.* San Francisco: Berrett-Koehler.

Renesch, J. (1994). *Leadership in a new era: Visionary approaches to the biggest crisis of our time.* San Francisco: New Leaders Press.

Rogers, R., Hayden, J., Ferketish, B., with Matzen, R. (1985). *Organizational change that works: How to merge culture and business strategies for maximum results.* Pittsburgh, PA: Development Dimensions International.

Ross, G. (1994). *Toppling the pyramids: Redefining the way companies are run.* New York: Times Books.

Russell, P. (1995). *The global brain awakens: Our next evolutionary leap.* Palo Alto, CA: Global Brain, Inc.

Ryan, K., & Oestreich, D. (1991). *Driving fear out of the workplace: How to overcome the invisible barriers to quality, productivity, and innovation.* San Francisco: Jossey-Bass.

Schein, E. (1969). *Process consultation: Its role in organization development.* Reading, MA: Addison-Wesley.

Schein, E. (1999). *The corporate culture survival guide: Sense and nonsense about culture change.* San Francisco: Jossey-Bass.

Schwartz, P. (1996). *The art of the long view.* New York: Doubleday.

Senge, P. (1990). *The fifth discipline: The art and practice of the learning organization.* New York: Doubleday.

Senge, P., Kleiner, A., Roberts, C., Ross, R., & Smith, B. (1994). *The fifth discipline fieldbook.* New York: Doubleday.

Senge, P., Kleiner, A., Roberts, C., Roth, G., Ross, R., & Smith, B. (1999). *The dance of change: The challenges of sustaining momentum in learning organizations.* New York: Doubleday.

Sheldrake, R. (1995). *A new science of life: The hypothesis of morphic resonance.* Rochester, VT: Park Street Press.

Singer, J. (1994). *Boundaries of the soul: The practice of Jung's psychology.* New York: Doubleday.

Smith, H. (1992). *Forgotten truth: The common vision of the world's religions.* San Francisco: HarperCollins.

Spencer, S.A., & Adams, J.D. (1990). *Life changes: Growing through personal transitions.* San Luis Obispo, CA: Impact Publishing.

Stacey, R.(1992). *Managing the unknowable: Strategic boundaries between order and chaos in organizations.* San Francisco: Jossey-Bass.

Talbot, M. (1986). *Beyond the quantum.* New York: Bantam.

Tart, C. (1975). *States of consciousness.* New York: E.P. Dutton.

Tichy, N., with Cohen, E. (1997). *The leadership engine: How winning companies build leaders at every level.* New York: HarperCollins.

Waldrop, M. (1992). *Complexity: The emerging science at the edge of order and chaos.* New York: Touchstone.

Walsh, R., & Vaughan, F. (1993). *Paths beyond ego: The transpersonal vision.* New York: Penguin/Putnam.

Waterman, R. (1987). *The renewal factor: How the best get and keep the competitive edge.* New York: Bantam.

Watkins, J.M., & Mohr, B. (2001). *Appreciative inquiry: Change at the speed of imagination.* San Francisco: Jossey-Bass/Pfeiffer.

Weisbord, M.R. (1978). *Organizational diagnosis: A workbook of theory and practice.* Reading, MA: Addison-Wesley.

Weisbord, M., & Janoff, S. (1995). *Future search: An action guide to finding common ground for action in organizations.* San Francisco: Berrett-Koehler.

Weisinger, H. (1998). *Emotional intelligence at work: The untapped edge for success.* San Francisco: Jossey-Bass.

Wheatley, M. (1994). *Leadership and the new science: Learning about organization from an orderly universe.* San Francisco: Berrett-Koehler.

Wheatley, M., & Kellner-Rogers, M. (1995). *A simpler way.* San Francisco: Berrett-Koehler.

Wilber, K. (1977). *The spectrum of consciousness.* Wheaton, IL: Theosophical Publishing House.

Wilber, K. (1982). *The holographic paradigm and other paradoxes.* Boston, MA: Shambhala.

Wilber, K. (1996). *A brief history of everything.* Boston, MA: Shambhala.

Wilber, K. (1998). *The marriage of sense and soul.* New York: Random House.

Wilber, K. (1999). *One taste: The journals of Ken Wilber.* Boston, MA: Shambhala.

Williamson, M. (1992). *Return to love.* New York: HarperCollins.

Wilson, J. (1994). *Leadership trapeze: Strategies for leadership in team-based organizations.* San Francisco: Jossey-Bass.

Wolf, F. (1988). *Parallel universes: The search for other worlds.* New York: Touchstone.

Wolf, F. (1989). *Taking the quantum leap: The new physics for nonscientists.* New York: Harper & Row.

Young, A. (1976). *The reflexive universe.* Englewood Cliffs, NJ: Prentice Hall.

Zukav, G. (1979). *The dancing Wu Li masters.* New York: Bantam.

About the Authors

Dean Anderson is co-founder and principal in the consulting and training firm, Being First, Inc. Mr. Anderson consults to Fortune 500 companies in transformational change, assisting them to build change strategy and develop executives, consultants, and project managers into change leaders. His current passion is helping his clients create enterprise-wide personal and cultural breakthroughs to a conscious way of being, working, and relating. In 1980, Mr. Anderson founded the Optimal Performance Institute, which was one of the first organizations in the country providing the pragmatics of self-mastery and personal change to organizational leaders.

Mr. Anderson created Being First's renown leadership breakthrough training, is the central developer of The Co-Creating System,™ and is co-author of Being First's comprehensive Change Tools. He authored the *Optimal Performance Manual* and

"Making Personal Change Trainings Work in Organizations," developed the Co-Creative Partnering and Team Development Process, and produced the *Self Mastery Series* audiotape program.

Mr. Anderson has two degrees from Stanford University, a bachelor of arts in communications and a master's degree in education.

Photo credit Jonas Grushkin/Photogenesis

Linda S. Ackerman Anderson is a co-founder and principal in the consulting and training company, Being First, Inc. She specializes in facilitating large-system change in Fortune 500 businesses and the military, particularly enterprise-wide transformational change. She is currently creating a curriculum for developing women executives called "Women As Leaders of Change." Over the past twenty-five years, her work has focused on change strategy development for transformational changes. In the past ten years, she and her partners have established themselves as thought leaders on facilitating conscious transformation and changing organizational mindset and culture as drivers of transformational change.

Ms. Ackerman Anderson was a founding creator of the organization transformation field, and chaired the Second International Symposium on Organization Transformation in 1984. To help define this field, she has published several articles, including "Development, Transition or Transformation: Bringing Change Leadership into the 21st Century"; "The Flow State: A New View of Organizations and Leadership"; and "Flow State Leadership in Action: Managing Organizational Energy."

In 1981, Ms. Ackerman Anderson formed Linda S. Ackerman, Inc., then merged it in 1988 with the Optimal Performance Institute, headed by Dean Anderson, to form Being First, Inc. Prior to forming her first business, Ms. Ackerman Anderson spent four years working at Sun Company, Inc., and one of its subsidiaries, Sun Petroleum Products Company, as both an organization development consultant and manager of human resources planning and development.

Ms. Ackerman Anderson's professional education includes Columbia University's Advanced Organization Development and Human Resources Management Program (1978–1979) and University Associates' Laboratory Education Internship

Program (1977–1978). She has served on the faculty for the UA Intern Program and other UA conferences and many university professional development programs.

Ms. Ackerman Anderson received her master's degree in interdisciplinary arts from Columbia University's Teachers College and her bachelor's degree in art history and education from Boston University.

For further information, contact:

Being First, Inc.
1242 Oak Drive, DW2
Durango, CO 81301
USA
(970) 385-5100 voice
(970) 385-7751 fax
www.beingfirst.com
email:danderson@beingfirst.com
        lindasaa@beingfirst.com

About the Editors

William J. Rothwell, Ph.D. is professor of human resource development in the College of Education at The Pennsylvania State University, University Park. He is also president of Rothwell and Associates, a private consulting firm that specializes in a broad array of organization development, human resource development, performance consulting and human resource management services.

Dr. Rothwell has authored, co-authored, edited, or co-edited numerous publications, including *Practicing Organization Development* (with R. Sullivan and G. McLean, Jossey-Bass/Pfeiffer, 1995). Dr. Rothwell's latest publications include *The ASTD Reference Guide to Workplace Learning and Performance*, 3rd ed., 2 vols. (with H. Sredi, HRD Press, 2000); *The Competency Toolkit*, 2 vols. (with D. Dubois, HRD Press, 2000); *Human Performance Improvement: Building Practitioner Competence* (with C. Hohne and S. King, Gulf Publishing, 2000); *The Complete Guide to Training Delivery: A Competency-Based*

223

Approach (with S. King and M. King, Amacom, 2000); *Building In-House Leadership and Management Development Programs* (with H. Kazanas, Quorum Books, 1999); *The Action Learning Guidebook* (Jossey-Bass/Pfeiffer, 1999); and *Mastering the Instructional Design Process,* 2nd ed. (with H. Kazanas, Jossey-Bass/Pfeiffer, 1998).

Dr. Rothwell's consulting client list includes thirty-two companies from the *Fortune* 500.

Roland Sullivan has worked as an organization development (OD) pioneer with nearly eight hundred organizations in ten countries and virtually every major industry.

Mr. Sullivan specializes in the science and art of systematic and systemic change, executive team building, and facilitating Whole System Transformation Conferences—large interactive meetings with from three hundred to fifteen hundred people.

Mr. Sullivan has taught courses in OD at seven universities, and his writings on OD have been widely published. With Dr. Rothwell and Dr. McLean, he was co-editor of *Practicing OD: A Consultant's Guide* (Jossey-Bass/Pfeiffer, 1995).

For over two decades, Mr. Sullivan has served as chair of the OD Institute's Committee to Define Knowledge and Skills for Competence in OD and was a recent recipient of the Outstanding OD Consultant of the World award from the OD Institute.

Mr. Sullivan's current professional learning is available at *www.RolandSullivan.com.*

Kristine Quade is an independent consultant who combines her background as an attorney with a master's degree in organization development from Pepperdine University, and years of experience as both an internal and external OD consultant.

Ms. Quade draws from experiences in guiding teams from divergent areas within corporations and across many levels of executives and employees. She has facilitated leadership alignment, culture change, support system alignment, quality process improvements, organizational redesign, and the creation of clear strategic intent that results in significant bottom-line results. A believer in whole systems change, she has developed the expertise to facilitate groups ranging in size from eight to two thousand in the same room for a three-day change process.

Recognized as the 1996 Minnesota Organization Development Practitioner of the Year, Ms. Quade teaches in the master's programs at Pepperdine University and the University of Minnesota at Mankato and the master's and doctoral programs at the University of St. Thomas in Minneapolis. She is a frequent presenter at the Organization Development National Conference and also at the International OD Congress and the International Association of Facilitators.

Index